CAMBRIDGE SCHOOL
Chaucer

THE
Franklin's
PROLOGUE AND TALE

Edited by Valerie Allen and David Kirkham

CAMBRIDGE
UNIVERSITY PRESS

The publishers would like to thank Professor Helen Cooper for her help in the preparation of this edition.

CAMBRIDGE UNIVERSITY PRESS
Cambridge, New York, Melbourne, Madrid, Cape Town, Singapore, São Paulo

Cambridge University Press
The Edinburgh Building, Cambridge CB2 2RU, UK

www.cambridge.org
Information on this title: www.cambridge.org/9780521666442

First published 2000
4th printing 2006

Printed in the United Kingdom at the University Press, Cambridge

A catalogue record for this publication is available from the British Library

ISBN-13 978-0-521-66644-2 paperback
ISBN-10 0-521-66644-9 paperback

Prepared for publication by Elizabeth Paren
Designed and formatted by Geoffrey Wadsley
Illustrated by Chris Price
Picture research by Valerie Mulcahy

Thanks are due to the following for permission to reproduce photographs:

The Bridgeman Art Library, London, pages 17,18 (Archivo Catedral de Tarazona/Index), 30 (British Library, London), 87 (British Museum, London); E.T. Archive/British Library, London, page 78; Mary Evans Picture Library, pages 48, 93; The Fotomas Index, page 50; Robert Harding Picture Library, pages 28 (Explorer), 46*l* (Mitch Diamond), 53 (Adam Woolfitt); Hulton Getty Picture Collection, pages 7, 13, 46*r*, 81, 85; Magnum Photos, page 79 (Jean Gaumy)

For cover photograph: Canterbury Tales: The Franklin's Tale, *Ellesmere Manuscript (Facsimile Edition 1911),* Private Collection/The Bridgeman Art Library, London

Contents

Introduction 5

What are The Canterbury Tales? 6

Chaucer's language 8

The Franklin's contribution 11

Text and notes

THE PORTRAIT OF THE FRANKLIN 12
(from The General Prologue)

THE FRANKLIN'S PROLOGUE 14

THE FRANKLIN'S TALE 18

Chaucer's pilgrims 78

Pilgrims and pilgrimages 80

Geoffrey Chaucer 82

Symbolism in the Franklin's Tale 84

Literary devices 85

The changing world of Chaucer's England 88

Gentillesse 90

Astronomy and astrology in the Franklin's Tale 92

Themes in the Franklin's Tale 95

Glossary of frequently-used words 96

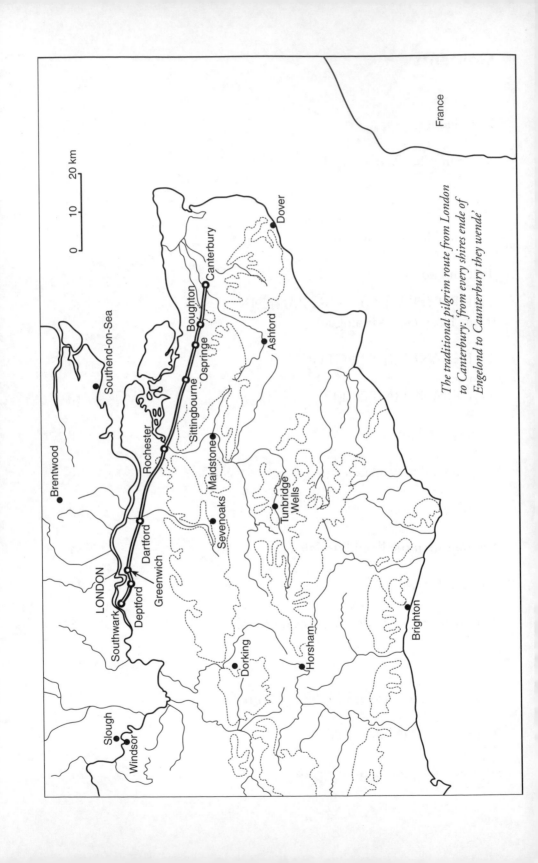

The traditional pilgrim route from London to Canterbury: 'from every shires ende of Engelond to Caunterbury they wende'

Introduction

The first encounter with a page of Chaucer in its original form can be a disconcerting experience. Initially, few words look familiar. Even when the meaning has been puzzled out, the reader is faced with an account of people who lived and died in a world very different from our own. The fourteenth century seems very far away, and you might be forgiven for thinking *The Canterbury Tales* are 'too difficult'.

The aim of this series is, therefore, to introduce you to the world of Chaucer in a way that will make medieval language and life as accessible as possible. With this in mind, we have adopted a layout in which each right-hand page of text is headed by a brief summary of content, and faced by a left-hand page offering a glossary of more difficult words and phrases as well as commentary notes dealing with style, characterisation and other relevant information. There are illustrations and suggestions for ways in which you might become involved in the text to help make it come alive.

If initial hurdles are lowered in this way, Chaucer's wit and irony, his ability to suggest character and caricature, and his delight in raising provocative and challenging issues from various standpoints, can more readily be appreciated and enjoyed. There is something peculiarly delightful in discovering that someone who lived six hundred years ago had a sense of humour and a grasp of personalities and relationships as fresh and relevant today as it was then.

Each tale provides material for fruitful discussion of fourteenth century attitudes and contemporary parallels. It is important to realise that the views expressed by the teller of any one tale are not necessarily Chaucer's own. Many of the activities suggested are intended to make you aware of the multiplicity of voices and attitudes in *The Canterbury Tales*. A considerable part of the enjoyment comes from awareness of the tongue-in-cheek presence of the author, who allows his characters to speak for themselves, thereby revealing their weaknesses and obsessions.

Essential information contained in each book includes a brief explanation of what *The Canterbury Tales* are, followed by hints on handling the language. There is then a brief introduction to the teller of the relevant story, his or her portrait from the General Prologue, and an initial investigation into the techniques Chaucer uses to present characters.

The left-hand page commentaries give information applicable to the text. Finally, each book offers a full list of pilgrims, further information on Chaucer's own life and works, some background history, and greater discussion of specific medieval issues. Suggestions for essays and themes to be explored are also included. On page 96 is a relatively short glossary of the words most frequently encountered in the text, to supplement the more detailed glossary on each page.

Chaucer's tales are witty, clever and approachable, and raise interesting parallels with life today. His manipulation of the short story form is masterly. We hope this edition brings *The Canterbury Tales* alive and allows you to appreciate Chaucer's art with ease and enjoyment.

What are The Canterbury Tales?

They are a collection of stories, loosely linked together, apparently told by a variety of storytellers with very different characters and from different social classes. In fact, both the storytellers themselves and the tales are the creation of one man, Geoffrey Chaucer. Chaucer imagines a group of pilgrims, setting off from the Tabard Inn one spring day on the long journey from London to the shrine of St Thomas à Becket in Canterbury – a journey that on horseback would take about four days.

To make time pass more pleasantly the pilgrims agree to tell stories to one another. Chaucer begins by introducing his pilgrims to the reader, in descriptions which do much to reveal the characters, vices and virtues of each individual. We learn more from the way each person introduces his or her tale, still more from the tales themselves and the way in which each one is told, and even further information is offered by the manner in which some pilgrims react to what others have to say. By this means Chaucer provides a witty, penetrating insight into the attitudes, weaknesses, virtues and preoccupations of English men and women of the fourteenth century. Some of their behaviour and interests may seem very strange to modern readers; at other times they seem just like us.

THE TALES

Although the complete text of *The Canterbury Tales* no longer exists, enough remains for us to appreciate the richness of texture and ironical comment Chaucer wove into his tapestry of fourteenth century life. The Tales themselves are quite simple – medieval audiences did not expect original plots, but rather clever or unexpected ways of telling stories that might be known in another form. Chaucer's audiences of educated friends, witty and urbane courtiers, perhaps the highest aristocracy, and even the king and queen, were clearly able to appreciate his skills to the full. Story telling was a leisurely process, since reading was a social rather than a private activity, and, since many people could not read, Chaucer would expect the Tales to be read aloud. You could try to read them like this – you will find advice on pronunciation on page 9 – and you will discover they become still more lively and dramatic when spoken rather than just read on the page.

Most of the Tales in the collection include aspects of at least one of the following categories of tales familiar to Chaucer's audience:

Courtly romances These stories of courtly love affairs were for the upper classes. They often told of unrequited love at a distance, the male lover suffering sleepless nights of anguish, pining away, writing poetry, serenading his beloved with love songs and performing brave feats of noble daring. Meanwhile the beloved (but untouchable) lady would sit in her bower and sew, walk in her castle gardens, set her lover impossible tasks to accomplish, and give him a scarf or handkerchief as a keepsake. Chaucer enjoys poking gentle fun at the rarefied atmosphere of such stories.

Fabliaux Extended jokes or tricks, often bawdy, and usually full of sexual innuendo.

The destination of the pilgrims – Canterbury Cathedral today

Fables Tales that make a moral point, often using animals as characters.

Sermons Sermons were stories with a moral message. Since 95 per cent of society could not read, sermons had to be good, interesting and full of dramatic storytelling. The line between a good story and a good sermon was very thin indeed. Usually there was an abstract theme (gluttony, avarice, pride) and much use was made of biblical and classical parallels or *exempla* to underline the preacher's point.

Confessions The storytellers often look back over their own lives, revealing faults and unhappinesses to the audience. This aspect is usually introduced in the teller's prologue to the actual story.

The Tales vary widely in content and tone, since medieval stories, Chaucer's included, were supposed both to instruct and entertain. Many have an underlying moral; some, such as the Pardoner's Tale, are also highly dramatic; and others, like those told by the Knight and the Squire, have their origins firmly in the courtly love tradition. But many are more complex than this suggests, for the way the tale is told often reflects the disposition and point of view of the teller: although the Nun's Priest's Tale claims to have a moral, it hardly justifies the great superstructure of the story; and the moral of the Pardoner's Tale is oddly at variance with the immorality of the teller.

The device of using different characters to tell different tales allows Chaucer to distance himself from what is being said, and to disguise the fact that he controls the varied and opinionated voices of his creations. He can pretend, for instance, to have no way of preventing the drunken Miller from telling his vulgar story about the carpenter's wife, and he can absolve himself from blame when the tellers become sexually explicit. A modern audience may find his frankness and openness about sex surprising, but it was understandable, for there was little privacy, even for the well-to-do, and sexual matters were no secret. The coarse satire of the fabliaux was as much enjoyed by Chaucer's 'gentil' audience as the more restrained romances.

7

Chaucer's language

The unfamiliar appearance of a page of Chaucerian English often prevents students from pursuing their investigations any further. It does no good telling them that this man used language with a complexity and subtlety not found in any writer of English anywhere before him. They remain unimpressed. He looks incomprehensible.

In fact, with a little help, it does not take very long to master Chaucer's language. Much of the vocabulary is the same as, or at least very similar to, words we use today. On page 96 there is a glossary of unfamiliar words most frequently used in this text, and these will quickly become familiar. Other words and phrases that could cause difficulties are explained on the page facing the actual text.

The language of Chaucer is known as Middle English – a term covering English as it was written and spoken in the period roughly between 1150 and 1500. It is difficult to be more precise than this, for Middle English itself was changing and developing throughout that period towards 'modern' English.

Old English (Anglo-Saxon) was spoken and written until around 1066, the time of the Norman Conquest. This event put power in England into the hands of the Norman lords, who spoke their own brand of Norman French. Inevitably this became the language of the upper classes. The effect was felt in the church, for speedily the control of the monasteries and nunneries was given to members of the new French-speaking aristocracy. Since these religious houses were the seats of learning and centres of literacy, the effect on language was considerable. If you were a wealthy Anglo-Saxon, eager to get on in the world of your new over-lords, you learnt French. Many people were bi- or even trilingual: French was the language of the law courts and much international commerce; Latin was the language of learning (from elementary schooling to the highest levels of scholarship) and the church (from parish church services to the great international institution of the papacy).

Gradually, as inter-marriage between Norman French and English families became more common, the distinction between the two groups and the two languages became blurred. Many French words became absorbed into Old English, making it more like the language we speak today. In the thirteenth century King John lost control of his Norman lands, and, as hostility between England and France grew, a sense of English nationalism strengthened. In 1362 the English language was used for the first time in an English parliament. At the same time, Geoffrey Chaucer, a young ex-prisoner of war, was sharpening his pens and his wit, testing the potential for amusement, satire and beauty in this rich, infinitely variable, complex literary tool.

Although some Tales are partly, or entirely, in prose, *The Canterbury Tales* are written largely in rhyming iambic couplets. This form of regular metre and rhyme is flexible enough to allow Chaucer to write in a range of styles. He uses the couplet form to imitate colloquial speech as easily as philosophical debate. Most importantly, Chaucer wrote poetry 'for the ear': it is written for the listener, as much as for the reader. Rhyme and alliteration add emphasis and link ideas and objects together in a way that is satisfying for the audience. The words jog along as easily and comfortably as the imaginary pilgrims and their horses jogged to Canterbury.

PRONUNCIATION

Chaucer spoke the language of London, of the king's court, but he was well aware of differences in dialect and vocabulary in other parts of the country. In the Reeve's Tale, for instance, he mocks the north country accents of two students. It is clear, therefore, that there were differences in pronunciation in the fourteenth century, just as there are today.

Having said that Chaucer wrote verse to be read aloud, students may be dismayed to find that they do not know how it should sound. There are two encouraging things to bear in mind. The first is that although scholars feel fairly sure they know something about how Middle English sounded, they cannot be certain, and a number of different readings can be heard, so no individual performance can be definitely 'wrong'. The second concerns the strong metrical and rhyming structure Chaucer employed in the writing of his Tales.

Finding the rhythm   Follow the rhythm of the verse (iambic pentameter), sounding or omitting the final 'e' syllable in the word as seems most appropriate. An 'e' before an 'h', for example, almost always disappears, as in the following:

> **His brother, which that knew of his penaunce,**
> **Up caught(e)　him, and to bedd(e)　he hath him broght,**

To sound the final 'e' at the end of 'caughte' or of 'bedde' in this case would be to add superfluous syllables. But in the case of this example:

> **Upon the morwe　whan that it was day,**
> **To Britaigne tooke they the righte　way**

the best swing to the regular ten-syllabled line is achieved by sounding the 'e' (as a neutral vowel sound, like the 'u' in put, or the 'a' in about) on the two occasions indicated.

Other points   In words beginning with the letter 'y' (for example, 'ywet', 'yknowe') the 'y' is sounded as it would be in the modern 'party'. Many consonants now silent were pronounced – as in 'knight', 'wrong'. All the consonants would be given voice in words such as 'neigheboures' and 'knight' and the 'gh' would be sounded like the Scots 'ch' in 'loch'. The combination 'ow' (for example, 'seistow', 'yow') is pronounced as in 'how', and the 'ei' in 'seist' would be like the 'a' sound in 'pay'.

For more ideas of what the language might have sounded like, listen to the tapes of Chaucer published by Cambridge University Press and the 'Chaucer Man' (Trevor Eaton).

WARM-UP ACTIVITIES

- Choose a long, self-contained section from the text: lines 89–133 provide a useful example, since the Franklin appears to be lecturing his audience, smugly and at considerable length, about the bliss of married life – a component of marriage many of them had clearly failed to find. After a brief explanation of the content, if considered necessary, students work in pairs, speaking alternately, and changing over at each punctuation point. It should be possible to develop a fair turn of speed without losing the sense of the passage.

- Again in pairs, choose about 10 lines of text; as one of the pair maintains a steady beat [^/^/^/^/^/] the partner does his or her best to fit the words to the rhythm.
- Choose a long self-contained unit from the text. Students walk round the room, speaking the script, and turning left or right at each punctuation mark. Dorigen's outburst about the black rocks (lines 193–221) is a good example of a speech that gives ample opportunity for a splendidly melodramatic interpretation. Another section for 'acting out' might be Aurelius' declaration of love, and Dorigen's initial response (lines 295–315).

GRAMMATICAL POINTS

Emphatic negatives   Whereas a person who stated that he 'wasn't going nowhere, not never' might be considered grammatically incorrect nowadays, Chaucer uses double or triple negatives quite often, to give a statement powerful added emphasis. One of the best known is in his description of the Knight in the General Prologue:

> **He never yet no vilenye ne sayde**
> **In al his life, unto no manner wight.**

Another occurs in the Franklin's Tale:

> **But they ne wiste why she thider wente.**
> **He nolde no wight tellen his entente.**

In both cases the multiple negatives strengthen the force of what is being said.

Word elision   In modern written English words and phrases are often run together (elided) to represent the spoken form of those words: didn't, can't, won't, I've and so on. Chaucer uses short forms of words too, usually when a character is speaking, and most frequently when he is using 'tow' meaning thou (you). Examples include the following:

seistow – you say	**wenestow?** – do you intend?
hastow – you have	**wostow why?** – do you know why?

The 'y' prefix   The past participle of a verb (particularly when the verb is passive) sometimes has a 'y' before the rest of the verb:

yblessed moot he be	he must be blessed
yflattered and yplesed	were flattered and pleased
her joly whistle wel ywet	her whistle had been well wet – i.e. she had had a great deal to drink.

The 'possessive' form of nouns   In modern English we indicate possession by means of an apostrophe: 'the hat of the man' becomes 'the man's hat'. Middle English had a particular formation that is still used in modern German – where we now use an apostrophe followed by an 's', Chaucer uses the suffix 'es'. So 'the man's hat' becomes 'the mannes hat' – the 'e' indicating that the word has two syllables.

The Franklin's contribution

In the General Prologue, the fascinating opening section to the Tales themselves, Chaucer introduces all the pilgrims, giving some idea of their status, personality and appearance. A list of the pilgrims who feature in the General Prologue may be found on page 78.

Significantly, he begins with those who are definitely at the top of the social scale. The Knight is a member of the aristocracy, the 'fighting class'; Chaucer begins with him and his party (his son, the Squire, and their Yeoman servant). He continues with a group of religious characters, all of whom have status and importance (the Prioress, the Monk and the Friar), moving through the social ranks, listing well-to-do middle class individuals, those of lesser wealth and influence, and ends with two unashamedly corrupt servants of the church, the Summoner and the Pardoner. This order of precedence is of particular significance to the Franklin, since he and his Tale are both passionately concerned with status and social standards.

The Franklin's place is in the midst of the group of well-to-do middle class, after the Merchant, and the Clerk. The word 'franklin' derives from the word 'franc' or 'free', and implied a landowner, often a wealthy one, but not a member of the noble or 'gentil' classes. He accompanies the Sergeant at Law and appears just before the Five Guildsmen. Chaucer offers copious details about the Sergeant at Law's acquisitions and abilities, but not much other information about him – suggesting that the man boastfully advertised his importance – and the Guildsmen with their status-conscious wives clearly consider themselves and their 'fraternity' to be of great consequence.

At first glance, the Franklin is less obviously concerned with personal status. He enjoys a good life, is cheerfully hospitable, and clearly expects a high standard from his servants. We are told that he is considered to be the 'Saint Julian' of his part of the country – a reputation that underlines his hospitality and might suggest he is the greatest landowner for many miles around. As such, he would naturally expect to be a person of some importance on the pilgrimage, but here he finds at least two people of greater social status – the Knight and his son, the Squire – and it is interesting to compare Chaucer's descriptions of these two characters with that of the Franklin. In the Franklin's Prologue, especially, Chaucer obtains wry social comedy from depicting a man anxious to prove that he is worthy of a high place on the social ladder. The tale Chaucer chooses to give him also seems appropriate. It is in the form of a Breton lay. These were spoken, rhymed stories of the type told in the courts of Brittany and were made popular in twelfth century England by the French poet, Marie de France. This may have seemed old-fashioned even in Chaucer's time, but the tale itself is derived from Boccaccio (who died in 1375), and was therefore very new. It is concerned with love in and out of marriage and the binding nature of promises. It also provides a 'happy' alternative to the views of marriage revealed in the tales of the Wife of Bath, the Clerk and the Merchant – an alternative intriguingly less perfect than the Franklin himself realises. Detailed discussion of the Breton lay, and courtly love, can be found on pages 86–7. Gentillesse, a code of behaviour associated with the gentry, is discussed on pages 90–2.

- Working with a partner, build up a picture of the life of the Franklin from these lines – his interests, his social position and his day-to-day activities. Does Chaucer give any hints about his character? What reason might he have for his pilgrimage?
- Write your own description of a man or woman of today, using Chaucer's method of building up character from small details of dress, habit and appearance.

333 **Frankeleyn** franklin [A 'free' man, a landowner – see note on page 91 for discussion of this man's social position.]

334 **Whit ... dayesye** his beard was as white as a daisy [a bright, sturdy, common plant]

335 **complexioun he was sangwin** he had a sanguine temperament [Medieval science believed human behaviour was dominated by the balance of four humours within each individual. The four character types were melancholic, choleric, phlegmatic and sanguine. A sanguine man could be recognised by a cheerful ruddy complexion, attractive appearance and outgoing personality.]

336 **by the morwe** first thing in the morning

336 **sop in wyn** bread dipped in wine [This was probably flavoured with almond milk, saffron, sugar, ginger, cinnamon and mace or nutmeg. Two meals a day were customary – midday dinner and supper in early evening. This is a little extra snack.]

338–40 **For he was ... felicitee parfit** he followed the teaching of Epicurus, who many thought encouraged ceaseless pursuit of pleasure as the route to happiness [This Athenian philosopher believed true pleasure came from pursuit of moral virtue, but his ideas were often distorted by pleasure-seekers. Chaucer suggests the Franklin is one of these, particularly in his enjoyment of food and wine.]

342 **Seint Julian** [patron saint of hospitality]

343 **alweys after oon** always top quality

344 **bettre envined ... nowher noon** nowhere could be found a man with better wines

345–6 **Withoute bake mete ... and flessh** his house never lacked cooked meats and fish

347–8 **It snewed ... koude thinke** it seemed to snow food and drink in his house ['Snow' suggests the exuberant excess of food associated with the Christmas season.]

349 **After the sondry sesons of the yeer** according to the various seasons of the year [It was not easy to preserve food, or obtain delicacies out of season.]

352 **breem ... in stuwe** bream and pike in his fishpond [a necessary addition to the larder in any large household]

353–4 **Wo was ... al his geere** it went badly for his cook if his sauces were not tasty and well-seasoned, or if he did not have everything in hand

355 **table dormant** the fixed, main table in the central hall [Trestles were otherwise used; the Franklin's table was always ready for entertaining.]

357–8 **At sessiouns ... of the shire** he had been chief magistrate in local courts, and represented his county in parliament [Chaucer was Knight of Shire for Kent in 1386.]

359 **gipser al of silk** a silk purse [so people notice his wealth]

361 **shirreve ... countour** sheriff and auditor of accounts for the county [the local big-wig]

The description of the Franklin from the General Prologue

A Frankeleyn was in his compaignye.
Whit was his berd as is the dayesye;
Of his complexioun he was sangwin.   335
Wel loved he by the morwe a sop in wyn;
To liven in delit was evere his wone,
For he was Epicurus owene sone,
That heeld opinioun that pleyn delit
Was verray felicitee parfit.   340
An housholdere, and that a greet, was he;
Seint Julian he was in his contree.
His breed, his ale, was alweys after oon;
A bettre envined man was nowher noon.
Withoute bake mete was nevere his hous   345
Of fissh and flessh, and that so plentevous,
It snewed in his hous of mete and drinke,
Of alle deyntees that men koude thinke.
After the sondry sesons of the yeer,
So chaunged he his mete and his soper.   350
Ful many a fat partrich hadde he in muwe,
And many a breem and many a luce in stuwe.
Wo was his cook but if his sauce were
Poynaunt and sharp, and redy al his geere.
His table dormant in his halle alway   355
Stood redy covered al the longe day.
At sessiouns ther was he lord and sire;
Ful ofte time he was knight of the shire.
An anlaas and a gipser al of silk
Heeng at his girdel, whit as morne milk.   360
A shirreve hadde he been, and a contour.
Was nowher swich a worthy vavasour.

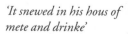

*'It snewed in his hous of
mete and drinke'*

- The Franklin successfully stops the flow of the Squire's story in mid-sentence. Take turns with a partner to read aloud lines 1–14 (up to 'As that ye been.') The Squire should attempt to continue a sentence that begins 'Apollo's chariot whirled into the sky and …' but must not be allowed to get any further. Discuss the Squire's feelings. Is he flattered by what is said about him or annoyed by the interruption?
- The question of 'gentility' is an important issue in the Franklin's tale, and is discussed more fully at the end of the book. List the qualities by which the Franklin suggests a 'gentil' man may be identified in these first 36 lines. Can gentility be detected in the way he speaks to both Squire and Host, as well as in what he says to them? Note particularly how he seems to confuse wealth with nobility.

1	**thou hast thee wel yquit** you have acquitted yourself well [put up a good performance]
4	**I allow the** I grant you [thee with one 'e' allows a rhyme with 'youthe']
5	**As to my doom** in my judgement
7	**good chaunce** good fortune
8	**in vertu … continuaunce!** may God grant you a life lived in manly virtue!
9	**of thy speche … deyntee** I have taken great pleasure from your words
11–4	**I hadde levere … that ye been** even if I had the chance of a parcel of land worth twenty pounds rent *per annum* ripe for the taking, I would sooner choose that my son was a man of discernment such as yourself
14–5	**Fy on … vertuous withal!** riches are nothing if a man lacks the noble qualities that should accompany them!
16	**snybbed** scolded
16	**yet shal** I shall do so again
17	**For he … entende** for he chooses to ignore the importance of noble behaviour

18	**pleye at dees** play dice [gamble]
18	**despende** waste money
19	**lese** lose
19	**usage** habit, custom
20	**hath levere** would prefer
20	**page** servant
22	**gentillesse** gentility [see page 90 for a full discussion of this]
23	**Straw for … oure Hoost** 'To the devil with gentility', said our Host ['To the devil with gentility!' is an approximation. Harry Baily, the bluff, outspoken landlord of the Tabard Inn where the pilgrims met, has joined them on their trip to Canterbury, and taken charge of organising the story-telling.]
24	**wel thou woost** you know well
24	**ech of yow** each of you
25	**moot … biheste** must tell at least one or two tales, or break his promise
28	**haveth … in desdeyn** don't take offence at my behaviour [a very polite phrase]

The Squire, who as the Knight's son is a member of the nobility, has been telling a tale about love and brave deeds; it seems to be endless, and the Franklin interrupts it here, with courtesy and skill. He curtails the Squire's ramblings, praises him, deplores the manners of his own son, and is urged by the Host to stop his fine talk and get on with his story.

'In feith, Squier, thow hast thee wel yquit
And gentilly. I preise wel thy wit,'
Quod the Frankeleyn, 'consideringe thy yowthe,
So feelingly thou spekest, sire, I allow the.
As to my doom, ther is noon that is heere   5
Of eloquence that shal be thy peere,
If that thou live; God yeve thee good chaunce,
And in vertu sende thee continuaunce!
For of thy speche I have greet deyntee.
I have a sone, and by the Trinitee,   10
I hadde levere than twenty pound worth lond,
Though it right now were fallen in myn hond,
He were a man of swich discrecioun
As that ye been. Fy on possessioun,
But if a man be vertuous withal!   15
I have my sone snybbed, and yet shal,
For he to vertu listeth nat entende;
But for to pleye at dees, and to despende
And lese al that he hath, is his usage.
And he hath levere talken with a page   20
Than to comune with any gentil wight
Where he mighte lerne gentillesse aright.'
  'Straw for youre gentillesse!' quod oure Hoost.
'What, Frankeleyn! pardee, sire, wel thou woost
That ech of yow moot tellen atte leste   25
A tale or two, or breken his biheste.'
  'That knowe I wel, sire,' quod the Frankeleyn.
'I prey yow, haveth me nat in desdeyn,
Though to this man I speke a word or two.'
  'Telle on thy tale withouten wordes mo.'   30

- The way a person speaks has always been one way in which an English person can tell which 'class' another comes from. Things were no different in the fourteenth century. Rhetoric was a skill linked to good breeding and education in good manners and conversational arts, which distinguished a 'gentil' man from a common person. By calling himself a 'burel' man, the Franklin is apparently denying his own claims to gentility; but in fact every word he speaks in lines 44–55 would be recognised as a rhetorical device by a discerning audience. On page 85 you will find a more detailed explanation of these devices, and how they are employed in this prologue and tale.
- When you have read the explanation, turn back to this page and consider how many times the Franklin repeats himself, in different words. Is such repetition effective? Does it add anything of importance? If not, why has Chaucer included these lines?
- Nowadays people tend to use rather pompous or showy language if they wish to impress others. Think of occasions when this occurs – after-dinner speeches, perhaps, formal letters of complaint, legal documents. Try to write the introductory paragraph to one such composition, bringing in as many pompous phrases and clichés as you can. (You might begin: 'My lords, ladies and gentlemen: unaccustomed as I am to public speaking …')

33–4	**I wol yow … wol suffise** I won't disobey you in any way, as far as I am able [very polite]	46	**rethorik** rhetoric [the art of public speaking]
37	**Britouns** Bretons	49	**Mount of Pernaso** Mount Parnassus [Supposed birthplace of the Muses, and by inference the source of inspiration for writers, artists and storytellers.]
38	**diverse aventures** various events		
38	**layes** lays [Narrative lays were short romances; they first appear in Anglo-Norman and French in the late twelfth and early thirteenth centuries, when they are said to derive from Breton legends. English lays appear later, but the form may well have appeared old-fashioned by the 1390s. The source here is in fact an Italian story by Boccaccio.]	50	**Ne learned … Scithero** nor learned ['the art of' is understood here] Marcus Tullius Cicero [the famous Roman orator]
		51–4	**Colours ne … to me queynte** I never learned anything about any 'colours', without doubt, except for the colours of nature, growing in the meadow, or the colours men use in dyeing or painting; the 'colours' of rhetoric are quite strange to me
41	**Or elles … hir plesaunce** or else read them for their pleasure		
43	**with good wil as I kan** as well as I can	55	**My spirit … swich mateere** my spirit knows nothing of such matters
43	**burel** plain, simple		
44	**I yow biseche** I beg you	56	**if yow liste** if you choose
45	**rude speche** uncouth way of talking		

With deliberately emphasised courtesy the Franklin starts his Tale. He says he knows an old-fashioned 'lay' (or spoken story) of the type told in the courts of Brittany. He protests that he is a simple man, unable to tell the story in a polished or educated manner.

'Gladly, sire Hoost,' quod he, 'I wole obeye
Unto your wil; now herkneth what I seye.
I wol yow nat contrarien in no wise
As fer as that my wittes wol suffise.
I prey to God that it may plesen yow;   35
Thanne woot I wel that it is good ynow.'
   Thise olde gentil Britouns in hir dayes
Of diverse aventures maden layes,
Rimeyed in hir firste Briton tonge;
Whiche layes with hir instrumentz they songe,   40
Or elles redden hem for hir plesaunce,
And oon of hem have I in remembraunce,
Which I shal seyn with good wil as I kan.
   But sires, by cause I am a burel man,
At my biginning first I yow biseche,   45
Have me excused of my rude speche.
I lerned nevere rethorik, certeyn;
Thing that I speke, it moot be bare and pleyn.
I sleep nevere on the Mount of Pernaso,
Ne lerned Marcus Tullius Scithero.   50
Colours ne knowe I none, withouten drede,
But swiche colours as growen in the mede,
Or elles swiche as men dye or peynte.
Colours of rethorik been to me queynte;
My spirit feeleth noght of swich mateere.   55
But if yow list, my tale shul ye heere.

The Franklin as depicted in the Ellesmere manuscript. This was written and decorated in the fifteenth century, but reproduced the style of dress of the 1380s

- What does the Franklin tell us about the knight and his lady here? You may wish to compare this knight's behaviour with that of the Knight and the Squire described in the General Prologue.
- The Franklin wishes to present an 'ideal' marriage, combining courtly love traditions with legal and practical marital relationships. There is further information on page 87 about the conventions associated with courtly love. How would the partnership normally change after the wedding day? Is there any evidence that the knight fears others might find this agreement strange or laughable?
- How much can you deduce about the Franklin's attitude to social status from the way he begins his tale?

57	**Armorik ... Britaine** Armorica, now called Brittany
58	**dide his paine** took great pains
59	**his beste wise** as best he could
60	**greet emprise** great enterprise
61	**oon the faireste** the most lovely one of all
63	**eek therto** what is more
63	**heigh kinrede** highborn family
64	**wel ... for drede** scarcely dared this knight, for fear
67	**meke obeisaunce** meek submissiveness
68	**penaunce** suffering
69–70	**prively she ... and hir lord** in private she made an agreement with him to take him as both her husband and her lord [For an explanation of the significance of this statement, see notes on courtly love conventions, page 87.]
75	**maistrie** mastery
76	**kithe hire jalousie** show jealousy towards her
79	**soverainetee** superiority, higher status
80	**for shame of his degree** out of regard for his position [both as a knight and as a husband]
82–3	**sith of youre gentillesse ... a reine** since your noble and courtly nature leads you to offer me such freedom and control

84–5	**Ne wolde ... werre or stryf** may God never allow hostility or discord between us through any fault of mine
87	**Have heere my trouthe** I give you my solemn oath [Use of the word 'trouthe' implies a most binding promise.]

'(She) hath swich a pitee caught of his penaunce
That prively she fil of his acord
To take him for hir housbonde and hir lord'

18

He sets his tale in Brittany. It is about a knight who woos and wins a beautiful, high-born lady to be his bride. He promises that after marriage he will continue to serve her humbly, instead of taking control over her as his wife.

In Armorik, that called is Britaine,
Ther was a knight that loved and dide his paine
To serve a lady in his beste wise;
And many a labour, many a greet emprise   60
He for his lady wroghte, er she were wonne.
For she was oon the faireste under sonne,
And eek therto comen of so heigh kinrede
That wel unnethes dorste this knight, for drede,
Telle hire his wo, his peyne, and his distresse.   65
But atte laste she, for his worthinesse,
And namely for his meke obeisaunce,
Hath swich a pitee caught of his penaunce
That prively she fil of his accord
To take him for hir housbonde and hir lord,   70
Of swich lordshipe as men han over hir wives.
And for to lede the moore in blisse hir lives,
Of his free wil he swoor hire as a knight
That nevere in al his lyf he, day ne night,
Ne sholde upon him take no maistrie   75
Again hir wil, ne kithe hire jalousie,
But hire obeye, and folwe hir wil in al,
As any lovere to his lady shal,
Save that the name of soverainetee,
That wolde he have for shame of his degree.   80
    She thanked him, and with ful greet humblesse
She seyde, 'Sire, sith of youre gentillesse
Ye profre me to have so large a reine,
Ne wolde nevere God bitwixe us tweyne,
As in my gilt, were outher werre or stryf.   85
Sire, I wol be youre humble trewe wyf,
Have heer my trouthe, til that myn herte breste.'
Thus been they bothe in quiete and in reste.

- Having proclaimed himself a 'burel' man with no rhetorical skills, the Franklin (perhaps unsurprisingly) employs the rhetorical device of digression in lines 89–114 to underline themes which will be significant in his story. Work out precisely what points he is making here. Do you agree with the suggestions he makes about human nature in general, and women in particular?
- Take particular note of his statement about the value of patience (lines 99–103), which is used by one character very successfully later in the tale, whilst others suffer for their lack of it.
- A number of important promises are made in the tale. Two occur in the last lines on this page. Does one seem more rash than the other?

89   **o thing … dar I seye** one thing, my lords, I can say with absolute confidence

90–1   **freendes … holden compaignye** lovers must give in to one another if they wish to stay together for long

92   **Love wole nat been constreyned by maistrye** love can't be forced by domination

96   **of kinde** by nature

97   **a thral** a slave

99–100   **Looke … al above** whoever is the most patient in love has the advantage over all others

102   **venquisseth** conquers

102   **thise clerkes seyn** these learned men tell us

103   **rigour** severity, discipline

104   **For every word … or pleyne** people can't make a fuss about every wrong word spoken

105–6   **Lerneth … or noon** learn to be tolerant, or, as I live, you'll have to learn to put up with things, whether you want to or not

108   **ne dooth or seith somtime amis** does not do or say something wrong at some time

109   **constellacioun** position of the planets [which was believed to have an effect on human behaviour]

110   **chaunginge of complexioun** balance of the 'humours' which affected one's disposition [The human body was influenced, so physicians believed, by four humours: phlegmatic, choleric, sanguine and melancholic, relating to the four 'juices' of the body – blood, phlegm, choler and bile. If the balance was upset in some way, a person felt 'ill-humoured' – 'out of sorts' physically or mentally.]

111   **doon amis or speken** do or say something amiss

112   **wreken** avenged

113–4   **After the time … governaunce** every person who understands self-control knows how to use restraint at certain times

116   **suffrance hir bihight** promised her forbearance

118   **defaute** fault

The Franklin pauses in his tale to comment on the nature of love and the importance of tolerance in any relationship, emphasising the promises this husband and wife have made to each other.

For o thing, sires, saufly dar I seye,
That freendes everich oother moot obeye,   90
If they wol longe holden compaignye.
Love wol nat been constreyned by maistrye.
Whan maistrie comth, the God of Love anon
Beteth his winges, and farewel, he is gon!
Love is a thing as any spirit free.   95
Wommen, of kinde, desiren libertee,
And nat to been constreyned as a thral;
And so doon men, if I sooth seyen shal.
Looke who that is moost pacient in love,
He is at his avantage al above.   100
Pacience is an heigh vertu, certeyn,
For it venquisseth, as thise clerkes seyn,
Thinges that rigour sholde nevere atteyne.
For every word men may nat chide or pleyne.
Lerneth to suffre, or elles, so moot I goon,   105
Ye shul it lerne, wher so ye wole or noon;
For in this world, certein, ther no wight is
That he ne dooth or seith somtime amis.
Ire, siknesse, or constellacioun,
Wyn, wo, or chaunginge of complexioun   110
Causeth ful ofte to doon amis or speken.
On every wrong a man may nat be wreken.
After the time moste be temperaunce
To every wight that kan on governaunce.
And therfore hath this wise, worthy knight,   115
To live in ese, suffrance hire bihight,
And she to him ful wisly gan to swere
That nevere sholde ther be defaute in here.

- The reader is being offered considerable information in these lines about the habits and attitudes of knights and their ladies – as interpreted by the Franklin. He repeats his explanation of the marriage arrangement, which would have seemed most unusual to a medieval audience. The nature of marriage is discussed in a number of the tales, notably those of the Merchant, the Wife of Bath, the Clerk and here the Franklin. All make a similar assumption – that one partner will normally have *maistrie* or dominance within the relationship. In spite of the fact that the courtly love conventions gave the lady power over her lover before marriage, social norms and current church teaching indicated that the husband was expected to be the dominant partner afterwards. The Franklin seeks to offer a relationship in which neither partner takes control – an idealised situation which is to be tested in the real world as the Tale unfolds.

- Discuss in a group or in pairs the Franklin's ideal explained in lines 119–26. Although unusual in the fourteenth century, does it seem more workable nowadays? How convincingly is the argument expressed? Do you feel that Chaucer, the author, is entirely in agreement with the Franklin, his creation, at this point?

- To what extent do you begin to feel that these characters are anything more than mere stereotypical figures at this point in the story? What do we learn about what is expected of knights in lines 127–41?

122	**servage** servitude
124	**sith** since
125	**certes** indeed
126	**The which … acordeth to** in accordance with the rules of the law of love
128	**Hoom … his contree** he went back to his homelands with his wife
129	**Pedmark** Penmarc'h [on the Breton coast, near Quimper]
130	**solas** comfort
131–3	**Who koude telle … and his wyf?** who can speak of the joy, benefit and prosperity that exists between husband and wife unless he himself has been married? [Echo of a similar sentiment expressed in The Merchant's Tale, there spoken in

bitter irony, but here to be taken literally.]

136	**of Kayrrud** [phonetic spelling of actual place named Kerru]
136	**was cleped Arveragus** was called Arveragus [Latin form of Celtic name; the fact he comes from a real place gives him individuality.]
137	**Shoop him** arranged
138	**cleped was eek Briteyne** also called Britain [In medieval times England was often called Great Britain and Brittany 'Little Britain' to distinguish them.]
140	**al his lust** all his enthusiasm
141	**the book** [The Franklin follows literary convention by pretending he has an ancient source for his tale.]

Having repeated his careful explanation of the unusual marriage arrangement between these two, the Franklin devotes a line or two to their state of marital bliss, before telling us that Arveragus, the Breton knight, finds it necessary to go adventuring to England for a year or two, seeking honour and fame.

Heere may men seen an humble, wys accord;
Thus hath she take hir servant and hir lord—   120
Servant in love, and lord in mariage.
Thanne was he bothe in lordshipe and servage.
Servage? nay, but in lordshipe above,
Sith he hath bothe his lady and his love;
His lady, certes, and his wyf also,   125
The which that lawe of love acordeth to.
And whan he was in this prosperitee,
Hoom with his wyf he gooth to his contree,
Nat fer fro Pedmark, ther his dwelling was,
Where as he liveth in blisse and in solas.   130
Who koude telle, but he hadde wedded be,
The joye, the ese, and the prosperitee
That is bitwixe an housbonde and his wyf?
A yeer and moore lasted this blisful lyf,
Til that the knight of which I speke of thus,   135
That of Kayrrud was cleped Arveragus,
Shoop him to goon and dwelle a yeer or tweyne
In Engelond, that cleped was eek Briteyne,
To seke in armes worshipe and honour;
For al his lust he sette in swich labour;
And dwelled there two yeer, the book seith thus.

- Courtly romances tended to concentrate on the brave deeds of knights-at-arms, but the Franklin instead turns his attention to the forlorn lady. Does his description of her activities in lines 145–9 seem artificial or realistic to you? How might you present Dorigen's behaviour here dramatically?
- The description of her grief agrees with the conventional method of expressing intense feeling in medieval poetry. Look again at the comment on line 146. What does this suggest about the narrator's knowledge of 'noble ladies'? What tone of voice would you use when making this statement out loud?
- We are told that Dorigen's grief is so extreme that it is comparable to a stone or rock which is only gradually affected by someone scratching it. Her frantic state is slightly improved by the kindly concern of her friends, but also by the letters telling her of Arveragus' welfare. What effect is Chaucer creating by mixing the artificial world of courtly romance with such touches of realism as the knight's letters home?
- After considering the points above, try writing a page of Dorigen's diary, or an exchange of letters between husband and wife.

142	**stynten** stop [talking]		155	**al hire bisinesse** all their efforts
144	**as hire hertes lyf** with all her heart		156	**hire hevinesse** her deep sorrow
145	**siketh** sighed		157–9	**By proces … emprented be** gradually, as you all know, men can carve away at a stone until eventually some impression is made upon it
146	**As doon … hem liketh** as these noble wives do when they choose			
147	**moorneth, waketh, waileth, fasteth, pleyneth** mourns, can't sleep, cries, fasts, laments		161	**resoun** reason [common sense]
148	**destreyneth** torments		162	**emprenting … consolacioun** some impression of their heartening words
149	**sette at noght** set at nought [considered worthless]		163–4	**grete sorwe … swich rage** her great sorrow began to abate; she could not go on for ever in such a passion
151	**in al that ever they may** in every way they could		168	**Or elles** otherwise
152	**prechen** begged		169	**slake** lessen
153	**causelees she sleeth hirself** she killed herself for no reason		171	**romen hire** stroll about
			172	**derke fantasye** terrible imaginings

Dorigen is left behind and full of woe. Her great grief gradually lessens, thanks to her concerned friends, and her husband's regular letters. Eventually friends persuade her to join their diversions.

Now wol I stynten of this Arveragus,
And speken I wole of Dorigen his wyf,
That loveth hire housbonde as hire hertes lyf.
For his absence wepeth she and siketh,   145
As doon thise noble wives whan hem liketh.
She moorneth, waketh, waileth, fasteth, pleyneth;
Desir of his presence hire so destreyneth
That al this wide world she sette at noght.
Hire freendes, whiche that knewe hir hevy thoght,   150
Conforten hire in al that ever they may.
They prechen hire, they telle hire night and day
That causelees she sleeth hirself, allas!
And every confort possible in this cas
They doon to hire with al hire bisinesse,   155
Al for to make hire leve hire hevinesse.
    By proces, as ye knowen everichoon,
Men may so longe graven in a stoon
Til som figure therinne emprented be.
So longe han they conforted hire, til she   160
Received hath, by hope and by resoun,
The emprenting of hire consolacioun,
Thurgh which hir grete sorwe gan aswage;
She may nat alwey duren in swich rage.
    And eek Arveragus, in al this care,   165
Hath sent hire lettres hoom of his welfare,
And that he wol come hastily again;
Or elles hadde this sorwe hir herte slain.
    Hire freendes sawe hir sorwe gan to slake,
And preyde hire on knees, for Goddes sake,   170
To come and romen hire in compaignye,
Awey to drive hire derke fantasye.
And finally she graunted that requeste,
For wel she saugh that it was for the beste.

- Clearly nothing can distract Dorigen from her melancholic fears about her lord. Do you consider her foolishly obsessive, or can love really be so deep that such fears are understandable? Whatever you decide, has she become more real to you than the figure described in lines 145–7?
- With a partner read out loud two short sections of Dorigen's speeches – lines 181–4 and 192–200. Try to bring out the different emotions through your reading. Which seems the more urgent and compelling to you? How does Chaucer use rhythm and vocabulary to emphasise the emotion Dorigen feels in each case?
- By suggesting that the rocks (and indeed there really are dangerous rocks off the coast of Brittany at Penmarc'h) are somehow unfair – an unnecessary and unpleasant addition to the universe – Dorigen is questioning God's ordering of the universe, something unacceptable in a learned male philosopher, and certainly unusual in a woman. Write down the main points of her argument, and discuss whether or not you agree with her. Are there aspects of life today that make people question ideas of divine order in the universe? Is it pointless to do so?

175	**castel** castle
175	**faste by** close by
177	**Hire to disporte** for her recreation
177	**bank an heigh** the high cliffs
178–9	**many a ship … liste go** she saw all sorts of ships and barges sailing on their way, wherever they chose to go
180	**a parcel of hire wo** a part of her misery
183–4	**Thanne were … smerte** then my heart would be quite healed of this bitter anguish
186	**caste … brinke** look down over the very edge of the cliff
187	**grisly rokkes blake** grim black rocks [Variations of this vivid phrase dominate subsequent lines, as the rocks themselves dominate Dorigen's thoughts.]
188–9	**verray feere … sustene** utter fear would make her heart tremble so much that she was unable to stand
191	**biholde** gaze

192	**sorweful sikes cold** sad, shivering sighs
193–5	**Eterne God … make** Eternal God, who through your providence directs this world with your infallible control, men say you made nothing without reason [These first lines sound like a conventional prayer: note the 'but' which comes next, and marks the beginning of her outburst.]
196	**feendly** devilish
197	**semen … confusion** seem rather an ugly muddle
199	**stable** unchangeable
200	**Why … unresonable?** why have you created such purposeless objects? [The rhythm of the verse, and the placing of this question so late in her speech, both emphasise the force of her outburst.]
202	**nis yfostred** is not benefited
202	**brid** bird
203	**anoyeth** causes distress

Walking along the cliff path, she would gaze at the ships sailing by and wish one carried her lord home again. At other times, she would look fearfully at the treacherous rocks and wonder why God had created them.

Now stood hire castel faste by the see,   175
And often with hire freendes walketh shee,
Hire to disporte, upon the bank an heigh,
Where as she many a ship and barge seigh
Seillinge hir cours, where as hem liste go.
But thanne was that a parcel of hire wo,   180
For to hirself ful ofte, 'Allas!' seith she,
'Is ther no ship, of so manye as I se,
Wol bringen hom my lord? Thanne were myn herte
Al warisshed of his bittre peynes smerte.'
    Another time ther wolde she sitte and thinke,   185
And caste hir eyen dounward fro the brinke.
But whan she saugh the grisly rokkes blake,
For verray feere so wolde hir herte quake
That on hire feet she mighte hire noght sustene.
Thanne wolde she sitte adoun upon the grene,   190
And pitously into the see biholde,
And seyn right thus, with sorweful sikes colde:
    'Eterne God, that thurgh thy purveiaunce
Ledest the world by certein governaunce,
In idel, as men seyn, ye no thing make.   195
But, Lord, thise grisly feendly rokkes blake,
That semen rather a foul confusion
Of werk than any fair creacion
Of swich a parfit wys God and a stable,
Why han ye wroght this werk unresonable?   200
For by this werk, south, north, ne west, ne eest,
Ther nis yfostred man, ne brid, ne beest;
It dooth no good, to my wit, but anoyeth.
Se ye nat, Lord, how mankinde it destroyeth?

- Learned churchmen would dispute eloquently and clearly before reaching their logical conclusion. Dorigen uses a similar pattern of speech, parodying their method and language in the way she brings her argument to a close. Remember, in the fourteenth century, men were dominant in all areas of learning, government and moral teaching. In this tale, the Franklin's two characters have already modified the normal pattern of marital power, by allowing the wife equality. As the story proceeds, the reader will be invited to judge whether or not such changes from the accepted order are beneficial. Dorigen's words here remind us that scholars tell us 'al is for the beste' – i.e. not to question what God has arranged. When the tale ends, consider if this seems to be proved by the way things fall out.

206	**al be they nat in minde** although they may have been forgotten
207–8	**Which mankinde … owene merk** this same mankind which is such a wonderful part of your creation that you made us in your own image
209	**greet chiertee** great tenderness
211	**swich meenes** such methods
213–5	**I woot … nat yknowe** I well know that scholars will say what they choose, by their various arguments, that everything that is, is for the best, even if I cannot understand the reason behind it [There is a hint here of the resentment of an ordinary person towards the lofty tone adopted by those who consider themselves to be superior. Do you think this reflects the Franklin's own position?]
216	**thilke God** by the same God
217	**as kepe my lorde!** may he keep my lord safe!
217	**this my conclusion** this is the conclusion I reach in my own argument
218	**lete I al disputison** I leave all the debating
225	**shopen for** made arrangements to
227	**places delitables** delightful spots
228	**ches and tables** chess and backgammon [Games popular with the leisured classes in both England and France.]

'But whan she saugh the grisly rokkes blake,
For verray feere so wolde hir herte quake'

28

Dorigen completes her argument, saying she cannot see the point of such rocks, and wishing they would disappear for her lord's sake. Her friends, seeing that cliff-walking is no comfort to her, offer alternative diversions.

An hundred thousand bodies of mankinde   205
Han rokkes slain, al be they nat in minde,
Which mankinde is so fair part of thy werk
That thou it madest lyk to thyn owene merk.
Thanne semed it ye hadde a greet chiertee
Toward mankinde; but how thanne may it bee   210
That ye swiche meenes make it to destroyen,
Whiche meenes do no good, but evere anoyen?
I woot wel clerkes wol seyn as hem leste,
By argumentz, that al is for the beste,
Though I ne kan the causes nat yknowe.   215
But thilke God that made wind to blowe
As kepe my lord! this my conclusion.
To clerkes lete I al disputison.
But wolde God that alle thise rokkes blake
Were sonken into helle for his sake!   220
Thise rokkes sleen myn herte for the feere.'
Thus wolde she seyn, with many a pitous teere.
   Hire freendes sawe that it was no disport
To romen by the see, but disconfort,
And shopen for to pleyen somwher elles.   225
They leden hire by riveres and by welles,
And eek in othere places delitables;
They dauncen, and they pleyen at ches and tables.

- The tale moves from the ugly mass of black rocks to a Maytime garden, full of flowers. Medieval castles frequently had gardens within the walls; and walled gardens were the traditional setting for stories of courtly love. Look carefully at the description of the garden on this page, and compare it with the black rocks described earlier. A detailed discussion of the two settings, their significance and symbolic importance, can be found on page 84.
- Working in pairs, use the text as a basis for some simple classroom drama. One person praises the beauty of the garden and the wonderful May weather, the other responds as Dorigen might have done. It is up to you to decide how successfully Dorigen is persuaded to enjoy herself.

229	**right in the morwe-tide** the very next morning	242	**Wold han maked** would have made
230	**ther biside** nearby	243–4	**but if to … in distresse** unless too much sickness or sorrow kept it in misery
231–2	**hadde maad … purveiaunce** had made arrangements for food and other provisions	235	**plesaunce** delight
235	**Which May** and May [The notion that follows of showers 'painting' the fresh colours of spring is common in medieval poetry and art.]	236	**after-diner** afternoon
		238	**Which made … hir moone** who maintained her complaint and lament
237	**craft of mannes hand** human skill [The garden is beauty created by man, but the jumbled black rocks were, puzzlingly, God's work.]	239	**ne saugh** never saw
		251	**nathelees … abide** nevertheless she must wait awhile
239	**swich prys** such value	252	**lete hir sorwe slide** give her sorrow a chance to lessen
240	**But if … paradis** unless it were paradise itself		

'The odour of floures and the fresshe sighte Wolde han maked any herte lighte'

They leave the rocky shoreline to picnic in a nearby garden where many sing and dance. Dorigen continues to regret her husband's absence, but does her best to be cheerful.

   So on a day, right in the morwe-tide,
Unto a gardyn that was ther biside,   230
In which that they hadde maad hir ordinaunce
Of vitaille and of oother purveiaunce,
They goon and pleye hem al the longe day.
And this was on the sixte morwe of May,
Which May hadde peynted with his softe shoures   235
This gardyn ful of leves and of floures;
And craft of mannes hand so curiously
Arrayed hadde this gardyn, trewely,
That nevere was ther gardyn of swich prys,
But if it were the verray paradis.   240
The odour of floures and the fresshe sighte
Wolde han maked any herte lighte
That evere was born, but if to greet siknesse,
Or to greet sorwe, helde it in distresse;
So ful it was of beautee with plesaunce.   245
At after-diner gonne they to daunce,
And singe also, save Dorigen allone,
Which made alwey hir compleint and hir moone,
For she ne saugh him on the daunce go
That was hir housbonde and hir love also.   250
But nathelees she moste a time abide,
And with good hope lete hir sorwe slide.

- The customs of courtly love offered an idealised pattern of behaviour to express thoughts and passions of real people. The description of Aurelius is in keeping with this idealised pattern, which required a young man to worship his beloved from afar, suffering secret pangs of unrequited love (especially if she was married to someone else). The tale now sets up an interesting situation, full of possibilities and tensions. If they were to maintain their courtly pattern of behaviour, Dorigen would continue bewailing her absent husband and Aurelius would suffer in silence. But one of Chaucer's intentions in this tale is to show how reality disrupts fantasy, something you might feel to be already evident within the story the Franklin tells. How do you think the story is likely to develop? Are both Dorigen and Aurelius foolish and self-indulgent in their separate longings and miseries?
- Working in small groups present a mime or a tableau of the situation as revealed in these lines, which expresses something of the inner feelings of those involved.
- We are told Aurelius wrote numerous songs and poems to his lady love. Create one or two of your own; they could be short ('Dorigen, Dorigen, When shall I see you again? I love you, I love you, Dorigen I am so blue'), or you could aim for a little more passion or sophistication. Remember he adores this married lady from afar. Does this seem likely to you? Can you imagine similar situations nowadays?
- What do the qualities given to Aurelius suggest about a young squire's lifestyle?

255–6	**fressher … of May** more fashionably and attractively dressed, I dare swear, than the month of May itself [Maytime was traditionally linked with courting and love and often illustrated in calendars by a picture of a fashionably dressed young man; this is a fine young gallant.]		272–3	**Save in … compleyning** only in songs he betrayed his misery as a sort of general lament
			275–6	**layes … virelayes** musical stories, formal laments [Chaucer himself wrote many of these and other short poems of set forms that could be set to music to accompany dancing.]
260	**Oon of … on live** one of the most handsome men alive		278	**langwissheth … helle** exists in helpless torment [Classical myth tells of Furies tormenting souls in Hell – here they are equally tormented – maybe Chaucer deliberately confuses the story.]
261	**right vertuous** talented			
262	**holden in greet prys** well regarded			
264	**Unwiting … at al** without Dorigen's knowledge			
265	**lusty** virile		279–80	**Ekko … Narcisus** [The nymph, Echo, was helplessly in love with Narcissus, as Aurelius is with Dorigen, thus implying his manly boldness has been reduced to effeminacy.]
265	**servant to Venus** [implies life dedicated to love]			
266	**ycleped** named			
268	**aventure** fortune [or misfortune]			
269–70	**nevere … his penaunce** never dared tell her of his misery but drained his cup of wretchedness to the bitter dregs		284	**observaunces** usual social events
			285	**swich a wise** such a way
			287	**wiste … entente** she knew nothing of his intentions

Aurelius, a handsome and noble young squire, is one of the group of dancers. Dorigen does not know he secretly loves her. His suffering is revealed only in his songs and verses.

Upon this daunce, amonges othere men,
Daunced a squier biforn Dorigen,
That fressher was and jolier of array,   255
As to my doom, than is the month of May.
He singeth, daunceth, passinge any man
That is, or was, sith that the world bigan.
Therwith he was, if men sholde him discrive,
Oon of the beste faringe man on live;   260
Yong, strong, right vertuous, and riche, and wys,
And wel biloved, and holden in greet prys.
And shortly, if the sothe I tellen shal,
Unwiting of this Dorigen at al,
This lusty squier, servant to Venus,   265
Which that ycleped was Aurelius,
Hadde loved hire best of any creature
Two yeer and moore, as was his aventure,
But nevere dorste he tellen hire his grevaunce.
Withouten coppe he drank al his penaunce.   270
He was despeyred; no thing dorste he seye,
Save in his songes somwhat wolde he wreye
His wo, as in a general compleyning;
He seyde he lovede, and was biloved no thing.
Of swich matere made he manye layes,   275
Songes, compleintes, roundels, virelayes,
How that he dorste nat his sorwe telle,
But langwissheth as a furye dooth in helle;
And die he moste, he seyde, as dide Ekko
For Narcisus, that dorste nat telle hir wo.   280
In oother manere than ye heere me seye,
Ne dorste he nat to hire his wo biwreye,
Save that, paraventure, somtime at daunces,
Ther yonge folk kepen hir observaunces,
It may wel be he looked on hir face   285
In swich a wise as man that asketh grace;
But nothing wiste she of his entente.

- Although the language he uses might seem strange nowadays, is this suggestion that 'being in love' is a miserable state to be in an idea that has gone out of date?
- Write or present various classroom improvisations showing a modern parallel to this moment when Aurelius discloses his love. Remember Aurelius snatches his opportunity in busy surroundings, with a backdrop of other people all enjoying themselves.
- Once again fantasy and reality become confused, as the conventions of romantic courtly love stories meet a real life situation. Young squires in love stories are bound to suffer pangs of unrequited and secret love for unattainable ladies; but as a married woman, Dorigen must refuse his advances, even if she loves him (does she?). Working with a partner, read out loud the conversation that takes place on this page. How closely do the two characters follow the idealised pattern of love here? Make a list of all the words and phrases that suggest honourable or noble behaviour and feelings. What emotions does Aurelius feel? And Dorigen?

288	**they thennes wente** they left that place
289–92	**By cause … in speche** because he was a neighbour, a respected and honourable man she had known for some time, they began to speak together
293	**drough** draw [nearer to the point of the conversation]
296	**So that I wiste** if I were to know
296	**glade** gladden
297	**wolde** wish
300–1	**wel I woot … myne herte** I know my devotion to you is hopeless; my reward will be merely heartbreak
302–3	**Madame … sleen or save** My lady, take pity on my bitter anguish; one word from you could kill or save me
304	**God wolde that I were grave** I pray God I might be buried
305	**leiser** time
306	**or ye wol do me deye** unless you want to kill me
307	**gan to looke** began to stare
308	**Is this youre wil** is this what you're after?
309	**Nevere erst** never before
310	**entente** intention
312	**Ne shal I nevere … wyf** I shall never ever be an untrue wife [double negative adds emphasis]
314	**to whom that I am knit** to whom I am bound

They happen to fall into conversation, and hesitantly Aurelius tells her of his love for her. At first she rejects him absolutely.

Nathelees it happed, er they thennes wente,
By cause that he was hire neighebour,
And was a man of worshipe and honour,   290
And hadde yknowen him of time yoore,
They fille in speche; and forth, moore and moore,
Unto his purpos drough Aurelius,
And whan he saugh his time, he seyde thus:
'Madame,' quod he, 'by God that this world made,   295
So that I wiste it mighte youre herte glade,
I wolde that day that youre Arveragus
Wente over the see, that I, Aurelius,
Hadde went ther nevere I sholde have come again.
For wel I woot my service is in vain;   300
My gerdon is but bresting of myn herte.
Madame, reweth upon my peynes smerte;
For with a word ye may me sleen or save.
Heere at youre feet God wolde that I were grave!
I ne have as now no leiser moore to seye;   305
Have mercy, sweete, or ye wol do me deye.'
She gan to looke upon Aurelius:
'Is this youre wil,' quod she, 'and sey ye thus?
Nevere erst,' quod she, 'ne wiste I what ye mente.
But now, Aurelie, I knowe youre entente,   310
By thilke God that yaf me soule and lyf,
Ne shal I nevere been untrewe wyf
In word ne werk, as fer as I have wit;
I wol been his to whom that I am knit.
Taak this for final answere as of me.'   315

- Dorigen makes a fatal mistake, which is to have widespread (and long-lasting) consequences. Her reply in lines 308–15 was decisive and perfectly correct, both morally and in accordance with courtly love conventions. What possible reason can she have for adding to it? After studying lines 317–33, one member of the class might volunteer to take the 'hot seat' as Dorigen, and explain her actions. Alternatively, the whole 'garden scene' offers an opportunity to look closely at language and characterisation through classroom improvisation.

- How effectively does Chaucer reveal his characters' emotions in this interchange? Is the reader expected to take their emotions seriously at all times? Using what is said and suggested in this entire garden scene, compose a diary entry for either Dorigen or Aurelius, indicating your thoughts, feelings and actions during the course of the day. Try to catch the 'tone' of feeling you have discerned in each character.

318–9	**Yet ... complaine** nevertheless I shall promise to be your love, since I see you lamenting so bitterly
320	**what day** on that day
320	**endelong** the whole length
322	**That they ... to goon** so that they do not prevent ships or boats from safely passing
324	**nis no stoon ysene** is no stone to be seen
326	**trouthe** solemn promise
326	**in al that evere I kan** to the best of my ability
327	**noon oother grace** no other mercy [he clearly feels this is an impossible task]

229	**shal never bitide** will never happen
330	**folies** foolishness
331	**what deyntee** what pleasure
332–3	**another mannes ... liketh** the wife of another man, able to enjoy her whenever he chooses
334	**soore siketh** sighed bitterly
337	**inpossible** impossibility
338	**moot I die ... horrible** must I die a ghastly and sudden death [Aurelius is being distinctly melodramatic here.]
339	**turned him anon** turned abruptly away

Then she impulsively offers him an apparently impossible task: if he can remove all the rocks from the Breton coast she will love him, she promises. This is her precondition, which she feels certain cannot be met. He should forget his love for her; she is a respectable married woman. Aurelius fears he will die in torment.

But after that in pley thus seyde she:
  'Aurelie,' quod she, 'by heighe God above,
Yet wolde I graunte yow to been youre love,
Sin I yow se so pitously complaine.
Looke what day that endelong Britaine   320
Ye remoeve alle the rokkes, stoon by stoon,
That they ne lette ship ne boot to goon,—
I seye, whan ye han maad the coost so clene
Of rokkes that ther nis no stoon ysene,
Thanne wol I love yow best of any man,   325
Have heer my trouthe, in al that evere I kan.'
  'Is ther noon oother grace in yow?' quod he.
  'No, by that Lord,' quod she, 'that maked me.
For wel I woot that it shal never bitide.
Lat swiche folies out of youre herte slide.   330
What deyntee sholde a man han in his lyf
For to go love another mannes wyf,
That hath hir body whan so that him liketh?'
  Aurelius ful ofte soore siketh;
Wo was Aurelie whan that he this herde,   335
And with a sorweful herte he thus answerde:
  'Madame,' quod he, 'this were an inpossible!
Thanne moot I die of sodeyn deth horrible.'
And with that word he turned him anon.

- The stark contrast between Aurelius' despair and the unthinking frivolity of his companions is clearly implied. Dorigen's rejection results in apparently hopeless suffering on the part of the young man. How would a modern writer try to describe his anguish? Working alone, or with a partner, write a modern parallel to this scene, beginning with Dorigen's rejection, at the end of line 339. (You might begin along the lines of: 'Abruptly he turned on his heel and walked away ...')
- Aurelius' prayer suggests the apparently deliberate confusion of pagan and Christian attitudes within the tale. Dorigen's earlier outburst seemed to address a recognisably Christian god, but here the squire appeals to other powers. What reasons can you find that make it seem appropriate to beseech Apollo? List as many as you can find. Other supernatural powers, such as astronomy and natural magic, feature later in the tale, and their merit is considered, directly by the Franklin, more subtly by Chaucer himself. The attitudes to religion, astronomy and magic are discussed briefly on page 92.

341	**in the aleyes romeden up and doun** strolled up and down the garden avenues	357	**pleynte** lament
		360	**flour** flower
342	**this conclusioun** the outcome [of this conversation]	361–2	**That yevest ... his seson** who gives to each plant its season of growth and flowering, according to your position in the heavens [Apollo, or Phoebus, the sun god, has the power of life over nature, and in seeking his help Aurelius is following his own natural instincts, rather than restraining them in accordance with moral or chivalric codes of behaviour.]
343	**revel** diversion		
344	**loste his hewe** lost its radiance		
345	**th'orisonte** the horizon		
345–6	**hath reft ... was night** had robbed the sun of light – in other words, night fell [The enchanting garden, apparently full of happy people, has contained at least two who suffer greatly.]		
		363	**herberwe** harbour, or position [in the sky]
347	**solas** delight	364	**merciable eighe** merciful eye
348	**save oonly** apart from	365	**lorn** desolate
349	**sorweful herte** heavy heart	367	**withoute gilt** through no fault of mine
350	**He seeth ... asterte** he saw there was no escape from his death [from hopeless love]	367	**but** unless
		367	**benignitee** compassion
353	**knowes bare** bare knees	369	**if yow lest** if you choose
353	**sette him doun** knelt down	370	**save my lady, best** apart from my lady, better than any other
354	**orisoun** prayers		
355	**for verray wo ... breyde** absolute despair sent him out of his mind	371	**devise** describe
		372	**in what wise** in what way
356	**niste** did not know [a contraction of 'ne wiste']		

The rest of the group continue to enjoy their holiday in the garden until nightfall. Aurelius alone returns home, heavy-hearted. In desperation he prays to Apollo, who, in his role of Phoebus the sun god, controls the world of growth and nature and the changing seasons. Only Apollo can help him.

Tho coome hir othere freendes many oon,   340
And in the aleyes romeden up and doun,
And nothing wiste of this conclusioun,
But sodeynly bigonne revel newe
Til that the brighte sonne loste his hewe;
For th'orisonte hath reft the sonne his light—   345
This is as muche to seye as it was night.
And hoom they goon in joye and in solas,
Save oonly wrecche Aurelius, allas!
He to his hous is goon with sorweful herte.
He seeth he may nat fro his deeth asterte;   350
Him semed that he felte his herte colde.
Up to the hevene his handes he gan holde,
And on his knowes bare he sette him doun,
And in his raving seyde his orisoun.
For verray wo out of his wit he breyde.   355
He niste what he spak, but thus he seyde;
With pitous herte his pleynt hath he bigonne
Unto the goddes, and first unto the sonne:
    He seyde, 'Appollo, god and governour
Of every plaunte, herbe, tree, and flour,   360
That yevest, after thy declinacion,
To ech of hem his time and his seson,
As thyn herberwe chaungeth lowe or heighe,
Lord Phebus, cast thy merciable eighe
On wrecche Aurelie, which that am but lorn.   365
Lo, lord! my lady hath my deeth ysworn
Withoute gilt, but thy benignitee
Upon my dedly herte have som pitee.
For wel I woot, lord Phebus, if yow lest,
Ye may me helpen, save my lady, best.   370
Now voucheth sauf that I may yow devise
How that I may been holpen and in what wise.

- Look carefully at the request Aurelius makes; he is not simply asking for the rocks to vanish, his request is much more complicated. In one sense it is in keeping with the rules of nature since he knows the movement of the sun affects the moon, and in turn the seas and high tides; in another what he wants is quite the opposite of these. This is not the first time a character has wished to break a set of rules. Make a note of when such a thing has occurred before, and the reason each character has had for his or her rebellion.
- The language Chaucer uses at this point is interesting. Are you made to feel that Aurelius really loves Dorigen? Or does he, rather childishly, simply want what he can't have? How much attention has he paid to Dorigen's wishes and feelings? Do they matter? Is such anguish and readiness to cause cosmic chaos purely for the sake of 'romantic love' self-indulgent or justifiable?

373–6	**Your blisful ... aboven him is she** your blessed sister, the bright goddess Lucina, chief ruler and queen of the seas (though Neptune is god of the sea, she is empress above him) [Lucina is also known as Diana]
377–81	**right as ... folwen hire** just as she longs to be quickened and set alight by your fire, Lord Apollo, which is why she follows you so persistently, in the same way the seas devotedly follow her [This explanation appropriately combines ideas of passionate sexual love and an understanding of the forces which control the movement of the planets and their effect on our natural world.]
382	**moore and lesse** great and small
384	**do myn herte breste** cause my heartbreak
385–6	**next at ... of the Leon** when sun and moon are next in opposition, which will be when the sun is in the house of Leo [in three months' time]
387	**As preieth hire** may it please her
388	**fadme** fathoms
388	**overspringe** rises above
390	**endure yeres tweyne** continue for two years

391	**certes** certainly
392	**holdeth your heste** keep your promise
392	**been aweye** have gone
394	**Preye hire ... than ye** beg her to travel no faster than you [He asks for the impossible and unnatural condition whereby the moon stays aligned with the sun in such a way as to cause a two-year high tide. To satisfy his desire for Dorigen, Aurelius is asking for cosmic chaos.]
397	**evene atte fulle alway** there will be perpetual full moon [and thus permanent high tides]
399	**but she vouche sauf in swich manere** if she will not consent through this action
402	**hir owene dirke regioun** [As Proserine, the moon goddess of classic myth inhabits the underworld, Dis]
406–7	**se the teeris ... som compassioun** see the tears on my cheek, and have pity on me
408	**swowne** swoon
408	**fil adoun** fell down

He asks Apollo to persuade the moon goddess to cause floods to submerge the rocks.

Youre blisful suster, Lucina the sheene,
That of the see is chief goddesse and queene
(Though Neptunus have deitee in the see,   375
Yet emperisse aboven him is she),
Ye knowen wel, lord, that right as hir desir
Is to be quiked and lighted of youre fir,
For which she folweth yow ful bisily,
Right so the see desireth naturelly   380
To folwen hire, as she that is goddesse
Bothe in the see and riveres moore and lesse.
Wherfore, lord Phebus, this is my requeste—
Do this miracle, or do myn herte breste—
That now next at this opposicion   385
Which in the signe shal be of the Leon,
As preieth hire so greet a flood to bringe
That five fadme at the leeste it overspringe
The hyeste rokke in Armorik Briteyne;
And lat this flood endure yeres tweyne.   390
Thanne certes to my lady may I seye,
"Holdeth youre heste, the rokkes been aweye."
    Lord Phebus, dooth this miracle for me.
Preye hire she go no faster cours than ye;
I seye, preyeth your suster that she go   395
No faster cours than ye thise yeres two.
Thanne shal she been evene atte fulle alway,
And spring flood laste bothe night and day.
And but she vouche sauf in swich manere
To graunte me my sovereyn lady deere,   400
Prey hire to sinken every rok adoun
Into hir owene dirke regioun
Under the ground, ther Pluto dwelleth inne,
Or nevere mo shal I my lady winne.
Thy temple in Delphos wol I barefoot seke.   405
Lord Phebus, se the teeris on my cheke,
And of my peyne have som compassioun.'
And with that word in swowne he fil adoun,
And longe time he lay forth in a traunce.

- What aspects of Arveragus and Dorigen, their characters and their relationship are stressed in lines 415–27? Why are these important to the narrative at this stage?
- Arveragus was away 'for a year or two', Aurelius had loved Dorigen for 'two years or more'. Now he takes to his bed for 'two years' at least. What effect on the mood of the story does such an casual measure of time have, in your view?
- The description of the arrow wound is a typical phrase for describing the anguish of secret love, and emphasises the misery and menace of such a passion. Chaucer's audience (many of them, like him, former combatants in England's war with France) would be well aware of the dangers of an arrow wound, outwardly healed but inwardly festering.

410	**penaunce** suffering	428	**sike** sick
411	**Dispeyred** in despair	431	**Er any … erthe gon** before he could put a foot on the ground
411	**thoght** obsession		
413–4	**Lete I … live or die** I shall leave this wretched creature lying there; he can choose for me whether to live or die [The author disclaims responsibility for his character, almost contemptuously.]	434	**werk** trouble
		437	**Under his breste … secree** beneath his heart he kept it more secretly
		438	**Pamphilus for Galathee** [Pamphilus and Galatea are characters in a slightly salacious medieval love poem: Pamphilus went to extreme lengths to persuade Galathea to have sex with him; Chaucer reminds us that Aurelius' romantic love has a sexual basis.]
415	**heele and greete honour** prosperity and great fame		
416	**of chivalrie the flour** the flower of chivalry [an outstandingly noble knight]		
418	**artow** art thou		
420	**fresshe** bold, vigorous [Chaucer stresses here the sexual aspect of love]	439–40	**His brest … arwe kene** his breast was undamaged to all appearances, but always in his heart was embedded that sharp arrow
422–4	**No thing … no doute** nothing prompted him to start wondering if anyone had spoken of love to her in his absence; he had no concerns about such a thing	441	**sursanure** a wound that has healed on the surface
		443	**But** unless
426	**daunceth … good cheere** danced, jousted, enjoyed himself		

Aurelius is tended by his brother, who knows his secret passion. Meanwhile, Arveragus returns
home safe and sound, and Dorigen is happy again. Aurelius endures tormenting pangs of
unrequited love for over two years, unable to leave his bed.

His brother, which that knew of his penaunce,   410
Up caughte him, and to bedde he hath him broght.
Dispeyred in this torment and this thoght
Lete I this woful creature lie;
Chese he, for me, wheither he wol live or die.
    Arveragus, with heele and greet honour,   415
As he that was of chivalrie the flour,
Is comen hoom, and othere worthy men.
O blisful artow now, thou Dorigen,
That hast thy lusty housbonde in thine armes,
The fresshe knyght, the worthy man of armes,   420
That loveth thee as his owene hertes lyf.
No thing list him to been imaginatif,
If any wight hadde spoke, whil he was oute,
To hire of love; he hadde of it no doute.
He noght entendeth to no swich mateere,   425
But daunceth, justeth, maketh hire good cheere;
And thus in joye and blisse I lete hem dwelle,
And of the sike Aurelius wol I telle.
    In langour and in torment furius
Two yeer and moore lay wrecche Aurelius,   430
Er any foot he mighte on erthe gon;
Ne confort in this time hadde he noon,
Save of his brother, which that was a clerk.
He knew of al this wo and al this werk;
For to noon oother creature, certeyn,   435
Of this matere he dorste no word seyn.
Under his brest he baar it moore secree
Than evere dide Pamphilus for Galathee.
His brest was hool, withoute for to sene,
But in his herte ay was the arwe kene.   440
And wel ye knowe that of a sursanure
In surgerye is perilous the cure,
But men mighte touche the arwe, or come therby.

The intervention of Aurelius' brother introduces an extra element of fantasy into the tale, emphasising the fact that Aurelius' love for Dorigen is somehow distanced from real life.

- With a partner consider how the magical displays described might have been achieved with the limited technological resources of the fourteenth century.
- Although the church condemned magic, common people's attitude to astrology was confused and the line between supernatural concerns and scientific knowledge was blurred. Astronomy was considered to be one of the highest forms of science, and there was firm belief in planetary influence on human life and behaviour. Look closely at the language used particularly in lines 451–62 and then lines 470–9. What is suggested about the Franklin's own attitude to magic?
- Few of Chaucer's tales emphasise the value of language in affecting our response to something or someone as clearly as this one. As the story progresses, you will notice that the status of the 'magician' changes. List the words used to describe him, and decide for yourself when and why the respect he is given alters.

445	**him fil in remembraunce** the memory occurred to him	
446	**Orliens** Orleans [students from Brittany, not part of France in the fourteenth century, frequently attended Orleans university]	
447–8	**lykerous … curious** eager to study unconventional and unusual matters [The words used suggest something rather unsavoury, preparing us for the Franklin's poor opinion of magic.]	
449	**every halke and every herne** every nook and cranny	
450	**Particular** peculiar	
452	**say** saw	
453	**magik natureel** natural or 'white' magic [as opposed to 'black magic']	
455–6	**Al were he … ylaft** although there to learn quite another skill, his friend ('felawe') had left this book surreptitiously on his desk	
457–9	**Which book … the moone** which book gave much detailed information about knowledge of changing	

positions of the moon in its 28-day orbit round the earth [and the effect these might have on our world]

459	**folye** foolishness
460	**nat worth a flye** not worth a fly [worthless]
461–2	**hooly … us to greve** our belief in the creed of the holy church prevents such illusions upsetting us
466	**warisshed hastily** quickly cured
467	**I am siker** I am sure
468	**diverse apparences** various illusions
469	**subtile tregetours** clever conjurers
470	**feestes** feasts
472	**a water** stream or river
474	**grim leoun** fierce lion
475	**floures … a mede** flowers spring up just as if in a meadow
477	**lym and stoon** mortar and stones
478	**whan hem liked** when they wished
478	**voided it anon** all at once it disappeared

Aurelius' grieving brother seeks help from a student of natural magic.

His brother weep and wailed prively,
Til atte laste him fil in remembraunce,   445
That whiles he was at Orliens in Fraunce,
As yonge clerkes, that been lykerous
To reden artes that been curious,
Seken in every halke and every herne
Particuler sciences for to lerne—   450
He him remembred that, upon a day,
At Orliens in studie a book he say
Of magik natureel, which his felawe,
That was that time a bacheler of lawe,
Al were he ther to lerne another craft,   455
Hadde prively upon his desk ylaft;
Which book spak muchel of the operaciouns
Touchinge the eighte and twenty mansiouns
That longen to the moone, and swich folye
As in oure dayes is nat worth a flye;   460
For hooly chirches feith in oure bileve
Ne suffreth noon illusioun us to greve.
And whan this book was in his remembraunce,
Anon for joye his herte gan to daunce,
And to himself he seyde prively: 465
'My brother shal be warisshed hastily;
For I am siker that ther be sciences
By whiche men make diverse apparences,
Swiche as thise subtile tregetoures pleye.
For ofte at feestes have I wel herd seye   470
That tregetours, withinne an halle large,
Have maad come in a water and a barge,
And in the halle rowen up and doun.
Somtime hath semed come a grim leoun;
And somtime floures springe as in a mede;   475
Somtime a vine, and grapes white and rede;
Somtime a castel, al of lym and stoon;
And whan hem liked, voided it anon.
Thus semed it to every mannes sighte.

- How does the 'magic' discussed in lines 482–8 differ from that in lines 470–9? Can magic be explained as an understanding of a particular set of rules – in this case, those governing natural sciences? Do you think that it would be fair to require Dorigen to keep her promise under these circumstances?
- 'he seyde a wonder thing' (line 503) sounds like the opinion of the narrator. What does it suggest about his reaction to magic and magicians, and how does this differ from the Franklin's stated opinion of magic revealed at an earlier stage? What other proof can you find of a discrepancy between what he says about magic, and his apparent reaction to it? More information about astrology and astronomy may be found on page 92.

482	**moones mansions** mansions of the moon [The 28 positions the moon occupies in the heavens during its 28-day cycle. Its influence on seas and tides, and astrologers believe on the lives of men, varies according to each position.]
483	**above** even more important
486	**mannes sight** the sight of man
489	**enduren a wowke or two** last a week or two [romantic love has become merely a quick fling]
490–2	**Thanne were ... atte leaste** then, if nothing else, she would be utterly shamed if she failed to keep her promise
493	**What sholde** why should
496	**stirte** started, jumped
498	**lissed** relieved
500	**furlong** [one-eighth of a mile]
502	**thriftily hem grette** greeted him politely

Humanity recognises both God and nature as forces governing the universe

The loving brother decides that if someone makes the rocks seem to disappear for a week or two Aurelius' cure is certain. He tells Aurelius of his plan, and together they instantly set out for Orleans. Before reaching the city a clerk meets them; amazingly, he is already aware of their objective.

    Now thanne conclude I thus, that if I mighte   480
At Orliens som oold felawe yfinde
That hadde thise moones mansions in minde,
Or oother magik natureel above,
He sholde wel make my brother han his love.
For with an apparence a clerk may make,   485
To mannes sighte, that alle the rokkes blake
Of Britaigne weren yvoided everichon,
And shippes by the brinke comen and gon,
And in swich forme enduren a wowke or two.
Thanne were my brother warisshed of his wo;   490
Thanne moste she nedes holden hire biheste,
Or elles he shal shame hire atte leeste.'
    What sholde I make a lenger tale of this?
Unto his brotheres bed he comen is,
And swich confort he yaf him for to gon   495
To Orliens that he up stirte anon,
And on his wey forthward thanne is he fare
In hope for to been lissed of his care.
    Whan they were come almoost to that citee,
But if it were a two furlong or thre,   500
A yong clerk rominge by himself they mette,
Which that in Latin thriftily hem grette,
And after that he seyde a wonder thing:
'I knowe,' quod he, 'the cause of youre coming.'
And er they ferther any foote wente,   505
He tolde hem al that was in hire entente.

- Note carefully the details of the show put on for Aurelius and his brother. In what ways would this particularly appeal to a young squire such as himself? Could it be interpreted as a warning to him? What effect would this show have on him?
- This is a useful moment to pause and consider the way in which the tale is being told. Does Chaucer remind the audience at this point of the personality of the Franklin narrator? Do some aspects of the story seem far more realistic and likely than others? Why should Chaucer choose to mix reality and fantasy in such a manner? Is he pointing out what happens when unreal romantic fantasy collides with real life?

509	**dede were** were dead [High mortality rates in the fourteenth century, partly as a result of the Black Death, meant that news of the deaths of many acquaintances would be upsetting but not surprising to the Franklin's audience.]
511	**lighte** alighted, jumped from
513	**maden hem wel at ese** made them very comfy
514	**lakked no vitaille** lacked no kind of food or drink
515–6	**So wel … nevere noon** Aurelius had never known a household so well supplied and furnished as this one in all his life
517	**sopeer** supper

519–20	**hertes with hir … with ye** harts with huge antlers, the largest seen by human eye
524–5	**fauconers … heron slain** falconers who used their hawks to kill heron by a beautiful river
526	**justing** jousting
527	**swich pleasaunce** such a pleasure
532	**ago** gone, vanished
536	**They setten stille, and no wight but they thre** they sat silent and motionless, no one else present but the three of them [The phrasing here suggests their stunned silence, and also emphasises the illusory nature of the scenes they had watched.]

'… saugh he knightes justing in a plain'

Aurelius' brother asks after old friends, and weeps to hear of their deaths. They are made most hospitably and comfortably welcome in the magician's house, and entertained with a show of magic.

This Briton clerk him asked of felawes
The whiche that he had knowe in olde dawes,
And he answerde him that they dede were,
For which he weep ful ofte many a teere.   510
    Doun of his hors Aurelius lighte anon,
And with this magicien forth is he gon
Hoom to his hous, and maden hem wel at ese.
Hem lakked no vitaille that mighte hem plese.
So wel arrayed hous as ther was oon   515
Aurelius in his lyf saugh nevere noon.
    He shewed him, er he wente to sopeer,
Forestes, parkes ful of wilde deer;
Ther saugh he hertes with hir hornes hye,
The gretteste that evere were seyn with ye.   520
He saugh of hem an hondred slain with houndes,
And somme with arwes blede of bittre woundes.
He saugh, whan voided were thise wilde deer,
Thise fauconers upon a fair river,
That with hir haukes han the heron slain.   525
    Tho saugh he knightes justing in a plain;
And after this he dide him swich plesaunce
That he him shewed his lady on a daunce,
On which himself he daunced, as him thoughte.
And whan this maister that this magik wroughte   530
Saugh it was time, he clapte his handes two,
And farewel! al oure revel was ago.
And yet remoeved they nevere out of the hous,
Whil they saugh al this sighte merveillous,
But in his studie, ther as his bookes be,   535
They seten stille, and no wight but they thre.

- Why should the magician be called 'maister' in line 537? Consider what lines 537–46 suggest about his personality – or that of the Franklin whose tale this is.
- What effect does the bargaining on the price of love have on the view that this is a tale of courtly love? Is this really such a romantic love affair? What precisely is Aurelius hoping for? The fact that the entire estate of a very wealthy merchant of Chaucer's time could be valued at £1000 merits consideration.
- Two more promises have been made in these lines. Decide exactly what has been promised, to whom, and make a note of it.
- How has the image of Aurelius been expanded and altered as the tale develops? Is Chaucer encouraging you to view him as a young hero – or something else?

538	**Is redy oure soper?** is our supper ready?	551	**made it straunge** held off, haggled
539	**undertake** dare swear	551	**so God him save** as he hoped for salvation
540	**Sith** since	552	**Lasse** less
542	**ther as my bookes be** where my books are kept	553	**Ne gladly ... nat goon** in fact he wasn't really happy to accept that sum
543–4	**whan it liketh ... right now** it's all ready, whenever you want it, right away if you like	555	**Fy on a thousand pound!** To the devil with a thousand pounds! [a very rash remark]
546	**Thise amorous folk ... han hir reste** these people in love have to take a break some time	558	**This bargain is ful drive, for we been knit** this bargain is settled, for we are agreed
547–8	**At after-soper ... gerdon be** after supper they began negotiations about what reward the master should be given	560–1	**But looketh ... to-morwe** but look here, don't be idle or lazy, let's not stay here any longer than tomorrow
550	**Gerounde ... Saine** [The Gironde and the Seine are two rivers to the north west and north east of Penmarc'h.]	562	**have heer my feith to borwe** take my promise as a pledge
		563	**whan him leste** when he chose
		566	**His woful ... a lisse** his wretched heart had release from its anguish

'Almoost an houre it is,
I undertake,
Sith I yow bad oure
soper for to make'

The magician, and owner of the house, summons his squire and orders supper to be served. Hard bargaining with Aurelius is resolved by a promise that the magician will remove all rocks in the vicinity of the Penmarc'h coast in return for £1000. Aurelius goes to bed a happy man, and sleeps soundly.

To him this maister called his squier,
And seyde him thus: 'Is redy oure soper?
Almoost an houre it is, I undertake,
Sith I yow bad oure soper for to make,   540
Whan that thise worthy men wenten with me
Into my studie, ther as my bookes be.'
    'Sire,' quod this squier, 'whan it liketh yow,
It is al redy, though ye wol right now.'
'Go we thanne soupe,' quod he, 'as for the beste.   545
Thise amorous folk somtime moote han hir reste.'
    At after-soper fille they in tretee
What somme sholde this maistres gerdon be,
To remoeven alle the rokkes of Britaine,
And eek from Gerounde to the mouth of Saine.   550
    He made it straunge, and swoor, so God him save,
Lasse than a thousand pound he wolde nat have,
Ne gladly for that somme he wolde nat goon.
    Aurelius, with blisful herte anoon,
Answerde thus: 'Fy on a thousand pound!   555
This wide world, which that men seye is round,
I wolde it yeve, if I were lord of it.
This bargain is ful drive, for we been knit.
Ye shal be payed trewely, by my trouthe!
But looketh now, for no necligence or slouthe   560
Ye tarie us heere no lenger than to-morwe.'
    'Nay,' quod this clerk, 'have heer my feith to borwe.'
    To bedde is goon Aurelius whan him leste,
And wel ny al that night he hadde his reste.
What for his labour and his hope of blisse,   565
His woful herte of penaunce hadde a lisse.

There is a pause in the tale at this point. Lines 573–83 present a word picture that stands out vividly from the narrative. Illuminated manuscripts in medieval calendars contained many similar visual images, showing the movement of planets and stars in the top part of the picture, and below these the actions of men on earth, dominated and influenced by what was happening above. This is an elaborate and rhetorical indication that these things took place in December, but more than this it makes oblique references to the events of the tale. Such images act as a reminder that earthly life is ruled by heavenly forces, but in this tale Aurelius would like the rules governing the forces of nature to be broken, so that he can satisfy his passion for Dorigen. The magician has shown him illusions that apparently defy the rules of nature, but we shall see that it is simply his understanding of these rules that allow him to make the rocks seem to disappear.

It would also be evident to Chaucer's original audience that this season of the year was associated with feasting, drinking and merriment, and specifically it was a period under the control of a Lord of Misrule, during whose 'reign' a certain licence and abandonment of the natural rules governing society was acceptable. However, once the year had turned, order was restored. Traditionally, too, the new year was the time when one expected to pay one's debts. It is therefore no accident that by this stage in the tale all promises have been made. It now remains to be seen which are kept and which broken.

570	**been descended … abide** dismounted at their destination
571	**remembre** remind
573–5	**Phebus wax old … stremes brighte** the old sun burnt like beaten copper, though during the hot summer months it was high in the sky, gleaming like burnished gold with brilliant rays
576	**in Capricorn adoun he lighte** it had moved into the sign of Capricorn [the sun had moved into Capricornus in December-January]
580	**Janus** [Janus is a mythical deity presiding over the turn of the year. He is a two-faced god, hence 'double beard'; January is named for him. Romans depicted him as sentinel at the main door of the house. Associated with Saturn, and the winter feasts of Saturnalia, as well as the twelve days of Christmas feasting suggested here, from December 25 to January 6th.]

581–3	**drinketh of … lusty man** drinks wine from his bugle horn [horn of a wild ox]; there before him stands the boar's head [traditional Christmas fare] and every good man cries out 'Nowel' [proclaiming Christ's birthday, from the Latin 'natalis']
584–6	**in al that … doon his diligence** in every way possible behaves pleasantly and courteously to this master, and begs him to do his utmost
587	**swerd** sword
589	**subtil** clever, crafty
589	**swich routhe** such pity
590–1	**spedde him … conclusioun** hastened to watch for a suitable time to complete his plans
593	**apparence or jogelrye** illusion or trick [text emphasises the change is illusory, not real]
594	**I ne kan** I don't know [but he does]
595	**wene and seye** believe and say

Aurelius and the magician set off for Brittany the next day. It was winter time, the sun in the sign of Capricorn, the turning of the year. Aurelius treated the magician with great courtesy, and he, in his turn, felt so sorry for the young man that he wasted no time in arranging for the rocks to disappear.

Upon the morwe, whan that it was day,
To Britaigne tooke they the righte way,
Aurelius and this magicien biside,
And been descended ther they wolde abide.　　570
And this was, as thise bookes me remembre,
The colde, frosty seson of Decembre.
　　Phebus wax old, and hewed lyk laton,
That in his hoote declinacion
Shoon as the burned gold with stremes brighte;　575
But now in Capricorn adoun he lighte,
Where as he shoon ful pale, I dar wel seyn.
The bittre frostes, with the sleet and reyn,
Destroyed hath the grene in every yerd.
Janus sit by the fyr, with double berd,　　580
And drinketh of his bugle horn the wyn;
Biforn him stant brawen of the tusked swyn,
And 'Nowel' crieth every lusty man.
　　Aurelius, in al that evere he kan,
Dooth to this maister chiere and reverence,　585
And preyeth him to doon his diligence
To bringen him out of his peynes smerte,
Or with a swerd that he wolde slitte his herte.
　　This subtil clerk swich routhe had of this man
That night and day he spedde him that he kan　590
To waiten a time of his conclusioun;
This is to seye, to maken illusioun,
By swich an apparence or jogelrye—
I ne kan no termes of astrologye—
That she and every wight sholde wene and seye　595
That of Britaigne the rokkes were aweye,
Or ellis they were sonken under grounde.

• The description of the magician's calculations is technically confusing. Calculations concerning celestial influences depended on the assumption that the heavenly bodies in the eighth sphere rotated more slowly than those in the ninth. Therefore, stars (such as Alnath) which had once been within a particular zodiacal sign, had moved out of alignment. Mathematical calculations were necessary to discover the precise time and place of the moon's greatest influence on the high tides off the Breton coast. Chaucer was interested in astronomy and informed; his audience would have been less familiar with the technical terms. Is the narrator being deliberately confusing here and, if so, why? Can you think of any modern parallels in which technical jargon might be used to impress an audience?

599 **japes and his wrecchednesse** tricks and wretched foolery

601 **tables Tolletanes** [Astronomical tables, drawn up in 1272 by order of king Alfonso of Castile, based on the longitude of Toledo. They were widely used by most medieval astronomers throughout Europe. The figures needed adjustment according to the whereabouts of the practitioner – in this case Brittany.]

602 **Ful wel corrected** carefully adjusted

602 **lakked noght** nothing was missing

603–4 **collect … expans yeeris … rootes** [Astrologers would begin their calculations with the *root* – the first date in the tables for which calculations were made. Tables for *collect* years allowed calculations for long periods of time, more precise definition was obtained from the tables for *expans* years. Study of a combination of these allowed calculation of a planet's position in a particular year.]

604 **othere geeris** other equipment

605–6 **centris … argumentz … proporcioneles convenientz** [Centres of the planets' circular movements, angles giving a planet's position in its own epicycle and figures for calculating positions of planets at given times.]

608 **eighte speer** eighth sphere [Medieval astrology embraced the ideas of Aristotle and Ptolemy that planets and sun circle round earth in nine concentric spheres, the whole system animated and ordered by the Prime Mover (Primum Mobile) beyond.]

609–12 **Alnath … al this** ['Fixed' stars, like Alnath (or Elneth) were in the eighth sphere. Constellations of the zodiac were represented as being in the ninth sphere, and gave fixed points of reference from which to make calculations.]

613 **firste mansioun** fixed position [That of Aries in the heavens. Aries was the constellation in which the sun crossed the celestial equator in springtime; all star positions were calculated from this point.]

614 **proporcioun** adjustment

616 **face, and terme** [Signs of the zodiac were divided into sections called faces and terms, which were ascribed to the influence of particular planets.]

616 **everydeel** every bit

617 **moones … operacioun** position of the moon appropriate to his proceedings

618 **observaunces** observations

620 **meschaunces** wicked, mischievous acts

621 **hethen** heathen

621 **thilke** those

622 **lenger** longer

623 **thurgh** through

Using complicated and detailed astrological calculations, described in impressive but baffling
detail, the clerk is finally able to achieve the illusion that, for a week or two, all the rocks have
disappeared.

So atte laste he hath his time yfounde
To maken his japes and his wrecchednesse
Of swich a supersticious cursednesse.   600
His tables Tolletanes forth he brought,
Ful wel corrected, ne ther lakked nought,
Neither his collect ne his expans yeeris,
Ne his rootes, ne his othere geeris,
As been his centris and his argumentz   605
And his proporcioneles convenientz
For his equacions in every thing.
And by his eighte speere in his wirking
He knew ful wel how fer Alnath was shove
Fro the heed of thilke fixe Aries above,   610
That in the ninthe specre considered is;
Ful subtilly he kalkuled al this.
   Whan he hadde founde his firste mansioun,
He knew the remenaunt by proporcioun,
And knew the arising of his moone weel,   615
And in whos face, and terme, and everydeel;
And knew ful weel the moones mansioun
Acordaunt to his operacioun,
And knew also his othere observaunces
For swiche illusiouns and swiche meschaunces
As hethen folk useden in thilke dayes.
For which no lenger maked he delayes,
But thurgh his magik, for a wyke or tweye,
It semed that alle the rokkes were aweye.

• Aurelius' words and behaviour deserve careful scrutiny at this point in the tale. At last he has achieved his aim. Remind yourself how long ago that first declaration of love for Dorigen took place. His behaviour to his 'master' (to whom he is now bound by a promise as imperative as Dorigen's to him) is respectful; his rush to find Dorigen reminds the audience that this is an impulsive young man; but how should we regard what he says to her? Make a note of the words that suggest how much he honours her, how painfully he adores her, and, particularly, why he is speaking to her. What change of tone do you detect in the last four lines? ('But of my deeth … by cause that I yow love.')

625–6	**which that … fare amis** who was still in despair, wondering whether his love would be granted to him, or whether things would go wrong	642	**nere it** if it were not [a negative]
		642	**disese** yearning, sorrow
		643	**moste dien … anon** could well die here at your feet, right now
628	**noon obstacle** no obstacle		
629	**voided … everichon** every rock had vanished	644	**Noght … wo bigon** I would not speak of my wretchedness
630	**fil anon** fell immediately	645	**certes** truly, indeed
632	**Venus** [this goddess reminds us this is sensual love]	645	**outher … or pleyne** I must either die or speak out [my anguished love]
633	**me han … cares colde** has relieved me of my chilling misery	646	**Ye sle me … peyne** You kill me, an innocent, guiltless man, with true misery [pain of love]
636	**anon-right** straight away	647	**of my deeth … routhe** even though you feel no pity for my death
637	**dredful herte** fearful heart		
637–8	**ful humble … lady deere** with great humility he greeted his adored sovereign lady	648	**Aviseth yow** take heed
		650	**me sleen … love** kill me because of my love for you
641	**lothest … displese** more reluctant to offend than any other person in the world		

Once he knows the rocks have vanished, Aurelius thanks the magician and immediately seeks out Dorigen. He accosts her with great humility, reminding her of his love and her promise.

Aurelius, which that yet despeired is   625
Wher he shal han his love or fare amis,
Awaiteth night and day on this miracle;
And whan he knew that ther was noon obstacle,
That voided were thise rokkes everichon,
Doun to his maistres feet he fil anon,   630
And seyde, 'I woful wrecche, Aurelius,
Thanke yow, lord, and lady myn Venus,
That me han holpen fro my cares colde.'
And to the temple his wey forth hath he holde,
Where as he knew he sholde his lady see.   635
And whan he saugh his time, anon-right hee,
With dredful herte and with ful humble cheere,
Salewed hath his soverein lady deere:
   'My righte lady,' quod this woful man,
'Whom I moost drede and love as I best kan,   640
And lothest were of al this world displese,
Nere it that I for yow have swich disese
That I moste dien heere at youre foot anon,
Noght wolde I telle how me is wo bigon.
But certes outher moste I die or pleyne;   645
Ye sle me giltelees for verray peyne.
But of my deeth thogh that ye have no routhe,
Aviseth yow er that ye breke youre trouthe.
Repenteth yow, for thilke God above,
Er ye me sleen by cause that I yow love.   650

- In order to consider the position of the two characters at this stage in the tale you might find it helpful to compose a diary entry for either Dorigen or Aurelius when you have considered the points below.
- Working carefully through Aurelius' speech, consider how the tone changes as the blackmail underneath the respectful words becomes clear. Why does he use the word 'right' so often? What is he threatening her with? What is he asking for? What has happened to 'love'?
- The tale has reached a point at which romance and Aurelius' adoration from afar has become entangled with reality. He now poses a real threat to Dorigen. Does Dorigen react in a way that seems realistic to you? The importance of Arveragus' absence becomes even more important in the lament which follows this, but is the audience already being offered an oblique comment on Dorigen's supposed 'freedom' and 'equality' within her marriage?

Once again the black rocks are the cause of Dorigen's lament – but notice that, ironically, it is the absence of rocks that she now considers as against natural order, rather than their presence.

651	**For, madame … han hight** for, madame, you know full well what you promised	667	**astoned** astounded
		668	**nas** was not
652	**chalange** claim	669	**wende nevere** had never believed
653	**grace** mercy or favour	672	**monstre or merveille** monstrous or fantastic thing
656	**youre trouthe plighten ye** you pledged your vow to me		
		673	**agains the proces of nature** contrary to the natural order of things
659–60	**I speke it … hertes lyf** I speak of this out of concern for your honour, rather than to save my own broken heart	675	**unnethe may she go** she could hardly walk
		677	**swowneth** fainted, swooned
662	**vouche sauf** consent or grant	677	**routhe** pity [read here as 'pitiable']
664	**quik or deed** alive or dead	678	**why it was** the reason for this
665	**In yow … or deye** you hold the power to give me life or death		

He reminds her of her solemn vow, and tells her the rocks have disappeared. As he walks away Dorigen is left pale and stupefied by this incredible news. She is in a pitiful state, with no-one to tell since Arveragus is absent.

For, madame, wel ye woot what ye han hight—
Nat that I chalange any thing of right
Of yow, my soverein lady, but youre grace—
But in a gardyn yond, at swich a place,
Ye woot right wel what ye bihighten me;   655
And in myn hand youre trouthe plighten ye
To love me best—God woot, ye seyde so,
Al be that I unworthy am therto.
Madame, I speke it for the honour of yow
Moore than to save myn hertes lyf right now,—   660
I have do so as ye comanded me;
And if ye vouche sauf, ye may go see.
Dooth as yow list; have youre biheste in minde,
For, quik or deed, right there ye shal me finde.
In yow lith al to do me live or deye,—   665
But wel I woot the rokkes been aweye.'
    He taketh his leve, and she astoned stood;
In al hir face nas a drope of blood.
She wende nevere han come in swich a trappe.
'Allas,' quod she, 'that evere this sholde happe!   670
For wende I nevere by possibilitee
That swich a monstre or merveille mighte be!
It is agains the proces of nature.'
And hoom she goth a sorweful creature;
For verray feere unnethe may she go.   675
She wepeth, wailleth, al a day or two,
And swowneth, that it routhe was to see.
But why it was to no wight tolde shee,
For out of towne was goon Arveragus.

- Dorigen's lament lasts for 100 lines and, Chaucer tells us, for 'a day or two'. It is undoubtedly a deliberate exaggeration of a traditional rhetorical device found in romantic literature of the time. It begins seriously enough. A noble woman's standing in the eyes of the world was based on her reputation for chastity and integrity, and Dorigen clearly sees death or dishonour as the only choices open to her. She recalls unhappy ladies of the past. Her list begins with a blood-curdling example – yet even at this early point there is a hint of humour in the melodramatic and absurd picture of a large number of secretly jumping virgins. As you read the lament ask yourself how the examples change, and also why Dorigen goes on for so long. Is Chaucer making points about a literary convention, about his heroine, about his narrator the Franklin, or perhaps all of these?

683   **pleyne** complain, lament

684   **unwar ... cheyne** all unaware I have been entangled in your chain [This expresses the idea of the wheel of Fortune, to which humanity is attached, turning from happiness to depths of sorrow through pure chance, not just deserts.]

685   **woot I no socour** I know of no means of assistance

687   **Oon of ... to chese** I must choose one of these two [she spells out her options very clearly]

688–90   **have I levere ... my name** I should prefer to lose my life than bring disgrace with my body, or know I have been false [broken a promise – but which one?], or have lost my reputation

691   **ywis** certainly

694   **doon trespas** commit some sinful act

695   **Yis, certes, lo** yes, certainly, look here [perhaps a suggestion of self-encouragement here]

696   **thritty tirauntz** thirty tyrants

697   **feste** feast

698   **t'areste** to be seized

699   **biforn hem in despit** before them in cruelty

700   **fulfille** satisfy

701   **fadres** father's

701   **God yeve hem meschaunce!** may God curse them [the tyrants]

703   **drede** apprehension

704   **Rather ... maidenhede** rather than lose their virginity

705–6   **prively ... dreynte hemselven** secretly jumped into a well and drowned themselves [After Sparta's victory over Athens in 404 BC, Phidon was overthrown and killed, and a reign of tyranny ensued.]

707–8   **of Mecene ... Lacedomye** men from Messene had enquiries and searches made in Lacedaemonia [Sparta]

709   **On which ... lecherye** upon whom they would perform lecherous deeds

710   **noon** not one

711–12   **nas ... maidenhede** was not one of them who was not killed, and who did not choose with right good will to die rather than agree to be forced to lose her virginity

She begins her long lament that Fortune should have put her in such a quandary; her only choice is between death and dishonour, and she considers women from the past who faced similar dilemmas.

But to hirself she spak, and seyde thus,   680
With face pale and with ful sorweful cheere,
In hire compleynt, as ye shal after heere:
  'Allas,' quod she, 'on thee, Fortune, I pleyne,
That unwar wrapped hast me in thy cheyne,
Fro which t'escape woot I no socour,   685
Save oonly deeth or elles dishonour;
Oon of thise two bihoveth me to chese.
But nathelees, yet have I levere to lese
My lyf than of my body to have a shame,
Or knowe myselven fals, or lese my name;   690
And with my deth I may be quit, ywis.
Hath ther nat many a noble wyf er this,
And many a maide, yslain hirself, allas!
Rather than with hir body doon trespas?
  Yis, certes, lo, thise stories beren witnesse: 695
Whan thritty tirauntz, ful of cursednesse,
Hadde slain Phidon in Atthenes attc fcstc,
They comanded his doghtres for t'areste,
And bringen hem biforn hem in despit,
Al naked, to fulfille hir foul delit,   700
And in hir fadres blood they made hem daunce
Upon the pavement, God yeve hem meschaunce!
For which thise woful maidens, ful of drede,
Rather than they wolde lese hir maidenhede,
They prively been stirt into a welle,   705
And dreynte hemselven, as the bookes telle.
  They of Mecene leete enquere and seke
Of Lacedomye fifty maidens eke,
On whiche they wolden doon hir lecherye.
But was ther noon of al that compaignye   710
That she nas slain, and with a good entente
Chees rather for to die than assente
To been oppressed of hir maidenhede.

- Dorigen's lament says there are 'more than a thousand' examples to be found in the wide range of classical and historical legends that would have been familiar to Chaucer, and to many in his courtly and sophisticated audience. You might wish to research further details of one or two of them, or re-tell one in your own words.

715 **Aristoclides** [tyrant ruler of Orchomenos in Arcadia]

716 **heet** named

718 **Dianes** [Diana was goddess of chastity]

718 **right** straight away

719 **hente** seized hold

721 **arace** tear away

723 **sith** since

723 **swich despit** such loathing

724 **defouled** degraded

724 **foul delit** bestial appetites

725 **Wel oght … slee** how much more readily then should a wife kill herself

727 **Hasdrubales wyf** the wife of Hasdrubal [King of Carthage at the time of its defeat by Rome at the end of the Third Punic War, 146 BC; he killed himself when Rome triumphed.]

728 **birafte hirself hir lyf** took her own life

729 **wan the toun** won the town

730–1 **skipte adoun … fyr** skipped down into the fire [rather a sprightly verb to use]

733 **Lucresse yslain hirself** Lucretia killed herself [but after her rape by Tarquin]

737 **Milesie** Miletus [overrun by the Gauls ('folk of Gawle') in 276 BC]

738 **verrey drede and wo** absolute fear and woe

738 **hem … oppresse** should rape them

740 **Mo** more

740 **as I gesse** I guess

741 **touching … mateere** about such things

742 **Habradate** Abradate [Susi king killed in battle against Egypt]

743–4 **Hirselven slow … and wide** killed herself, letting her blood flow into Habradates' deep wounds

745–6 **My body … if I may** no person shall defile my body in the slightest way, if it is within my power to prevent it

She feels the brave examples of such maidens should encourage a wife to escape similar dishonour
by death, and says there are plenty of models to choose from.

Why sholde I thanne to die been in drede?
Lo, eek, the tiraunt Aristoclides, 715
That loved a maiden, heet Stymphalides,
Whan that hir fader slain was on a night,
Unto Dianes temple goth she right,
And hente the image in hir handes two,
Fro which image wolde she nevere go. 720
No wight ne mighte hir handes of it arace
Til she was slain, right in the selve place.
   Now sith that maidens hadden swich despit
To been defouled with mannes foul delit,
Wel oghte a wyf rather hirselven slee 725
Than be defouled, as it thinketh me.
What shal I seyn of Hasdrubales wyf,
That at Cartage birafte hirself hir lyf?
For whan she saugh that Romayns wan the toun,
She took hir children alle, and skipte adoun 730
Into the fyr, and chees rather to die
Than any Romayn dide hire vileynye.
Hath nat Lucresse yslain hirself, allas!
At Rome, whan that she oppressed was
Of Tarquin, for hire thoughte it was a shame 735
To liven whan that she had lost hir name?
The sevene maidens of Milesie also
Han slain hemself, for verrey drede and wo,
Rather than folk of Gawle hem sholde oppresse.
Mo than a thousand stories, as I gesse, 740
Koude I now telle as touchinge this mateere.
Whan Habradate was slain, his wyf so deere
Hirselven slow, and leet hir blood to glide
In Habradates woundes depe and wide,
And seyde, "My body, at the leeste way, 745
Ther shal no wight defoulen, if I may."

- As you work through this list of great (and unfortunate) ladies of the past, make a note of why and how they died, how much is said about each one, and how relevant each example seems to be to Dorigen's situation. Is she elevating herself to heroic status? Or is the effect of this long list somewhat different? What are you expecting her to do when she has finished lamenting?
- How does Chaucer manipulate the reader's response to this character's predicament by the way she voices her 'lament'?

747–8 **What sholde ... hemselven slain** Why should I need to cite more examples of this, since so many have killed themselves

749 **Wel rather** much preferring this

750 **bet** better

754 **Demociones doghter deere** Demotion's dear daughter [who killed herself after her betrothed lover had died, rather than marry another man]

756 **Cedasus** Scedasus of Boetia [Plutarch tells how his daughters killed each other to avoid rape]

759 **As greet ... wel more** it was just as tragic, or even more so

760 **Nichanore** Nicanor [An officer in Alexander's army; after he conquered Thebes (336 BC), one Theban virgin killed herself rather than submit to his advances.]

762 **righte so** just the same

763 **oon of Macedonye** a man from Macedonia

764 **hir maidenhede redressed** avenged her lost virginity

765 **Nicerates wyf** wife of Niceratus [She killed herself after the murder of her husband by the Thirty Tyrants of Athens, lest she should be taken by them. In spite of Dorigen's assertion that this is a 'similar' case to her own, it seems quite different from her plight.]

767 **Alcebiades** Alcibiades [Athenian statesman assassinated in 404 BC whose mistress, Timandra, was killed for giving his body decent burial.]

She repeats her determination to kill herself, bolstering up her intention with an even more diverse list of noble ladies.

What sholde I mo ensamples heerof sayn,
Sith that so manye han hemselven slain
Wel rather than they wolde defouled be?
I wol conclude that it is bet for me   750
To sleen myself than been defouled thus.
I wol be trewe unto Arveragus,
Or rather sleen myself in som manere,
As dide Demociones doghter deere
By cause that she wolde nat defouled be.   755
O Cedasus, it is ful greet pitee
To reden how thy doghtren deyde, allas!
That slowe hemself for swich a manere cas.
As greet a pitee was it, or wel moore,
The Theban maiden that for Nichanore   760
Hirselven slow, right for swich manere wo.
Another Theban maiden dide right so;
For oon of Macidonye hadde hire oppressed,
She with hire deeth hir maidenhede redressed.
What shal I seye of Nicerates wyf,   765
That for swich cas birafte hirself hir lyf?
How trewe eek was to Alcebiades
His love, that rather for to dien chees
Than for to suffre his body unburied be.

- Dorigen's list of examples becomes increasingly agitated and ludicrously irrelevant. To gain a better idea of its absurdity, try a dramatic reading of the whole list (or a part of it), changing readers at each new example, and adopting a note of frantic self-persuasion. Dorigen is clearly trying to adopt the noble behaviour favoured by legendary women, but reality is not like this. Instead of a dramatic suicide, she hangs on (with increasing desperation) until her husband comes home, and then passes the problem over to him. Does this seem more like real life to you? Look back to the unusual marriage arrangement this couple made in the early part of the tale – are the promises made then being kept?
- Arveragus' reply seems to surprise his wife – is it the way you would have expected him to react?

770 **Alceste** Alcestis [Esteemed as a model of wifely excellence in the fourteenth century; she had chosen to die in place of her husband, Admetus. There is no need to repeat the well-known tale, which had already featured in Chaucer's earlier work *The Legend of Good Women*.]

771 **Omer** Homer [The *Odyssey* tells of Penelope's long wait for the return of her husband, Odysseus, and her steadfast refusal of a long line of suitors during his absence.]

773 **Laodamya** Laodamia [Her husband, Protesilaus, a Greek warrior, was killed by Hector during the Trojan siege; she chose to join Protesilaus in the underworld.]

776 **Porcia** Portia [Wife of Brutus; she killed herself through anxiety over her husband after his involvement in the assassination of Julius Caesar.]

778 **al hool hir herte yive** given her whole heart

779 **Arthemesie** Artemisia [She honoured her dead husband, Mausolus, by building him a splendid tomb, or mausoleum – hardly relevant to Dorigen's present plight.]

780 **Barbarie** barbarian lands

781 **Teuta** [unmarried queen of Illyria 241 BC]

783 **Bilyea** Bilia [of renowned chastity, she endured the bad breath of her husband, Dullius]

784 **Rodogone ... Valeria** Rhodogune [Daughter of Darius; she killed the nurse who tried to persuade her into a second marriage. Valeria also refused to marry a second time.]

786 **Purposing ever** always intending [is this true?]

787 **thridde** third

793–4 **al as ye ... yow namoore** everything you have already heard; there's no need to go through it again [Is it possible the audience feared the narrator would allow Dorigen to start again?]

795 **glad chiere** cheerful expression

796 **as ... yow devise** as I shall relate to you

797 **Is ther ... but this?** Is there anything else, Dorigen, apart from this?

798–9 **God help ... Goddes wille** God help me, this is far too much already

The long list ends with an incongruous collection of ladies, famous for a wide-ranging set of reasons. Her lament is cut short by the return of her husband, Arveragus. To him Dorigen pours out the whole story. His response is surprisingly restrained.

Lo, which a wyf was Alceste,' quod she.   770
'What seith Omer of goode Penalopee?
Al Grece knoweth of hire chastitee.
Pardee, of Laodomya is writen thus,
That whan at Troie was slain Protheselaus,
Ne lenger wolde she live after his day.   775
The same of noble Porcia telle I may;
Withoute Brutus koude she nat live,
To whom she hadde al hool hir herte yive.
The parfit wyfhod of Arthemesie
Honured is thurgh al the Barbarie.   780
O Teuta, queene! thy wyfly chastitee
To alle wives may a mirour bee.
The same thing I seye of Bilyea,
Of Rodogone, and eek Valeria.'
    Thus pleyned Dorigen a day or tweye,   785
Purposinge evere that she wolde deye.
But nathelees, upon the thridde night,
Hoom cam Arveragus, this worthy knight,
And asked hire why that she weep so soore;
And she gan wepen ever lenger the moore.   790
'Allas,' quod she, 'that evere was I born!
Thus have I seyd,' quod she, 'thus have I sworn'—
And toold him al as ye han herd bifore;
It nedeth nat reherce it yow namoore.
This housbonde, with glad chiere, in freendly wise   795
Answerde and seyde as I shal yow devise:
'Is ther oght elles, Dorigen, but this?'
    'Nay, nay,' quod she, 'God helpe me so as wys!
This is to muche, and it were Goddes wille.'

- In some ways this is the most intriguing section of the tale. Why does Arveragus choose to behave in this way? Why does the Franklin choose to tell a story that reaches such a surprising climax? What reasons might there be behind his choice? And, finally, what about the puppet master Chaucer himself? Is he, perhaps, pointing out how uncomfortably codes of idealistic behaviour fit into real life situations? The code of chivalry demanded that a 'trouthe' or promise made by a gentleman or lady could only be broken at the expense of one's honourable reputation. The marriage vows insisted that man and wife should be faithful to one another, and infidelity in a wife would mean the loss of her good name. Dorigen's foolish, impulsive promise to Aurelius, so long ago, means that one of these vows must be broken if the other is maintained.
- Does Arveragus' decision seem sensible or realistic to you? Look closely at his behaviour and his words in this section, and discuss whether or not you feel sympathetic towards him. Why, for instance, does he weep?
- It would certainly have been a fascinating mission for the two servants. Imagine how they might have gossiped and discussed what they knew of the situation as they trailed along behind the woeful Dorigen.

800–1	**Ye wife … yet to day** indeed, wife, it's no use agonising over old troubles. It may still happen that things may work out all right now
802	**by my fay** by my faith [I swear]
803	**so wisly** in his wisdom
804–6	**I hadde wel … kepe and save** I would rather be stabbed to death for the true love I bear you than that you should fail to keep and preserve your promise
807	**Trouthe … may kepe** a promise is the greatest and most binding contract one can make
808	**brast … wepe** immediately burst out crying
809	**up peyne of deeth** on pain of death
810	**while … ne breeth** while you have life or breath
811	**aventure** adventure, mischance
813–4	**Ne make … harm or gesse** nor show grief in my countenance, so that no person may guess or imagine any ill thing of you
819	**thider** thither
820	**nolde** did not wish [a negative]
821	**heep of yow** many of you
821	**ywis** indeed
822	**a lewed man** a coarse man [deliberately contrasted with 'gentleman']
823	**putte … in jupartie** put his wife in a position of such [moral] peril
825	**than yow semeth** than you imagine
826	**whan … demeth** make up your minds when you have heard the full story

Arveragus insists that she must keep her promise, in spite of the grief this will cause both of them.
He says she must tell no-one of this decision, and immediately summons a squire and
maidservant to accompany her on her road. The Franklin feels his audience may criticise the
knight for his decision, but cautions them to listen to the whole story before they judge him.

'Ye, wyf,' quod he, 'lat slepen that is stille.   800
It may be wel, paraventure, yet to day.
Ye shul youre trouthe holden, by my fay!
For God so wisly have mercy upon me,
I hadde wel levere ystiked for to be
For verray love which that I to yow have,   805
But if ye sholde youre trouthe kepe and save.
Trouthe is the hyeste thing that man may kepe'—
But with that word he brast anon to wepe,
And seyde, 'I yow forbede, up peyne of deeth,
That nevere, whil thee lasteth lyf ne breeth,   810
To no wight telle thou of this aventure—
As I may best, I wol my wo endure—
Ne make no contenance of hevinesse,
That folk of yow may demen harm or gesse.'
  And forth he cleped a squier and a maide: 815
'Gooth forth anon with Dorigen,' he saide,
'And bringeth hire to swich a place anon.'
They take hir leve, and on hir wey they gon,
But they ne wiste why she thider wente.
He nolde no wight tellen his entente.   820
  Paraventure an heep of yow, ywis,
Wol holden him a lewed man in this
That he wol putte his wyf in jupartie.
Herkneth the tale er ye upon hire crie.
She may have bettre fortune than yow semeth;   825
And whan that ye han herd the tale, demeth.

- Although Dorigen is going to keep her appointment with Aurelius in the garden (scene of her original promise to him and traditional setting for lovers' meetings), Chaucer tells us that they meet in the middle of a busy street, full of the everyday transactions of ordinary life. Is this important?
- Take particular note of Dorigen's words in line 840, and discuss how her marriage has changed since the opening of the tale.
- The narrator explains carefully why Aurelius renounces his claim on Dorigen. What has been most important in bringing about this change in him? Is the relative status of Arveragus and Aurelius (knight and squire) significant?

830	**right in the quikkeste strete** right in the busiest street	849–52	**Consideringe … alle gentillesse** if you considered what would be best in the circumstances it was better for him to put up with his lustful feelings than to perform a squalid, churlish and unworthy act in the face of such noble generosity and courtly behaviour [The language used stresses the contrast between chivalrous, gentlemanly behaviour and that associated with vulgar, base folk, suggesting ideals of 'gentillesse' are linked to suppression of physical, selfish appetites.]
831	**bown** prepared		
832	**ther as she had hight** just as she had promised		
833	**was to the gardyn-ward also** was also making his way to the garden		
834	**wel he spied** he certainly noticed		
836	**aventure or grace** by chance or good luck		
837	**saleweth … entente** greeted her in hopeful anticipation		
842	**gan wondren on this cas** felt surprised at this [line 825 had hinted at a surprise ending]	855	**sith I se** since I see
843–4	**hadde greet … lamentacioun** felt great pity for her and her lamentations	857–60	**That him were … bitwix yow two** rather than allow him to be humiliated (which would be a great pity) I think it would be better for me to endure my misery for ever. Better this than that I should disrupt the love between you two [such courtly formality emphasises the high-flown sentiments proclaimed]
847	**So looth … hir trouthe** he was so anxious that she should not break her promise		
848	**caughte of this greet routhe** was filled with immense sympathy		

Aurelius and Dorigen meet in the street as she is on the way to keep her promise to him. He is so impressed by the worthiness of the knight and overcome with pity for her that he releases her from her vow.

This squier, which that highte Aurelius,
On Dorigen that was so amorus,
Of aventure happed hire to meete
Amidde the toun, right in the quikkest strete,   830
As she was bown to goon the wey forth right
Toward the gardyn ther as she had hight.
And he was to the gardyn-ward also;
For wel he spied whan she wolde go
Out of hir hous to any maner place.   835
But thus they mette, of aventure or grace,
And he saleweth hire with glad entente,
And asked of hire whiderward she wente;
And she answerde, half as she were mad,
'Unto the gardyn, as myn housbonde bad,   840
My trouthe for to holde, allas! allas!'
   Aurelius gan wondren on this cas,
And in his herte hadde greet compassioun
Of hire and of hire lamentacioun,
And of Arveragus, the worthy knight,   845
That bad hire holden al that she had hight,
So looth him was his wyf sholde breke hir trouthe;
And in his herte he caughte of this greet routhe,
Consideringe the beste on every side,
That fro his lust yet were him levere abide   850
Than doon so heigh a cherlissh wrecchednesse
Agains franchise and alle gentillesse;
For which in fewe wordes seyde he thus:
  'Madame, seyth to youre lord Arveragus
That sith I se his grete gentillesse   855
To yow, and eek I se wel youre distresse,
That him were levere han shame (and that were routhe)
Than ye to me sholde breke thus youre trouthe,
I have wel levere evere to suffre wo
Than I departe the love bitwix yow two.   860

71

- This meeting takes place in a busy street – how would passers-by view it? And imagine the reactions of the two servants escorting Dorigen. How would they report what they had seen and heard when they returned to the castle?
- As a magistrate and sheriff the Franklin would have been very familiar with the language of the law and its power. The formal, legal language used by Aurelius in releasing Dorigen from her promise emphasises the importance of such a pledge. He makes a final promise himself in lines 865 and 866. What is your impression of his character and behaviour at this point? If he has renounced his claim to his love, what is he thinking of instead?

After renouncing Dorigen, for the first time Aurelius is forced to think of the consequences of the promise he himself made to pay £1000; romantic love is now eclipsed by financial necessity.

861–4 **I yow relesse … ye were born** I release you, madam, and discharge into your hands every oath and bond that you made me before this, since the day of your birth [The legal language of medieval quitclaim, familiar to a knight of the shire, such as the Franklin or Chaucer himself.]

865–6 **shal yow … biheste** shall never reproach you about any promise made

869–70 **every wyf … atte leeste** every wife should take care when making promises and remember Dorigen, at the very least

872 **withouten drede** without doubt

873 **thonketh** thanked

876 **be ye siker** you may be sure

876 **so weel apayd** so well rewarded

878 **What sholde … endite?** What point is there in spending any longer on their story?

880 **soverein blisse** total rapture

881 **Nevere eft … bitwene** there were never ever harsh words between them ever after [The use of double negative emphasises the point.]

884 **ye gete of me namoore** you get no more information from me

885 **cost al hath forlorn** had spent all his resources

888 **pured gold** pure gold

888 **of wighte** in weight [a very large fortune]

889 **philosophre** wise man, scholar [Although philosophers were popularly believed to be capable of turning base metal into gold – as in the 'philosopher's stone' – this shows more respect than 'magician', or even 'clerk'.]

890 **I se … fordo** I see no more but that I am ruined

Aurelius ceremonially releases her from her binding pledge, and she thanks him, returning happily to her husband. But Aurelius still owes £1000 to the magician – which he cannot pay.

I yow relesse, madame, into youre hond
Quit every serement and every bond
That ye han maad to me as heerbiforn,
Sith thilke time which that ye were born.
My trouthe I plighte, I shal yow never repreve   865
Of no biheste, and heere I take my leve,
As of the treweste and the beste wyf
That evere yet I knew in al my lyf.
But every wyf be war of hire biheeste!
On Dorigen remembreth, atte leeste.   870
Thus kan a squier doon a gentil dede
As wel as kan a knight, withouten drede.'
    She thonketh him upon hir knees al bare,
And hoom unto hir housbonde is she fare,
And tolde him al, as ye han herd me said;   875
And be ye siker, he was so weel apayd
That it were inpossible me to write.
What sholde I lenger of this cas endite?
    Arveragus and Dorigen his wyf
In soverein blisse leden forth hir lyf.   880
Nevere eft ne was ther angre hem bitwene.
He cherisseth hire as though she were a queene,
And she was to him trewe for everemoore.
Of thise two folk ye gete of me namoore.
    Aurelius, that his cost hath al forlorn,   885
Curseth the time that evere he was born:
'Allas,' quod he, 'allas, that I bihighte
Of pured gold a thousand pound of wighte
Unto this philosophre! How shal I do?
I se namoore but that I am fordo.   890

- What options face Aurelius now? Notice that an important issue is how his rash promise will affect the reputation of his family, just as Dorigen's affected the reputation of her husband. Wealth and good name are closely linked. In order to be considered a man of 'gentillesse' in the fourteenth century one had to not only to behave in a noble manner, but also possess sufficient wealth to maintain the appropriate standard of living. Spiritual and romantic considerations have been submerged by more worldly pressures. Is this something that still happens today?

- The manner in which Aurelius speaks to the man to whom he owes so much money tells us a great deal. Remember, when first introduced, he was simply a 'clerk', or even a 'tregetour' or charlatan. Now he is a philosopher and, in line 904, a 'master'. Is this a comment on the value of money?

891	**heritage** inheritance
891	**moot I nedes** I shall have to
892	**been** become
893–4	**shamen … bettre grace** bring shame upon all my family in this area, unless I can get some more merciful arrangement from him [the magician]
895	**wole of him assaye** will try to get an agreement from him
899	**cofre** chest [A strongbox in which a person's valuables would customarily be stored.]
902	**him bisecheth … gentillesse** beg him out of his nobility of nature [Gentillesse is an interesting word to use here to describe someone who is not a knight.]
903	**dayes of the remenaunt** some time to pay off the rest

904–5	**dar well … as yit** I can truly boast I have never yet failed to keep my word
906	**sikerly** certainly
907	**howevere that I fare** whatever happens to me
908	**To goon … kirtle bare** even if I go begging, bare-legged [maybe a touch of melodrama here]
909–11	**wolde ye … were I wel** if you would guarantee me a respite of two or three years, with security, then I could manage
911	**elles** otherwise
915	**holden covenant** kept my promise
917	**hastow nat** have you not
918	**sorwefully he siketh** he sighed bitterly

With ruin staring him in the face, Aurelius takes what gold he has and asks for time to pay the
rest of the debt, promising that this will be done within a few years. When he learns that
Aurelius has not enjoyed Dorigen's favours after all, the magician requests an explanation.

Myn heritage moot I nedes selle,
And been a beggere; heere may I nat dwelle,
And shamen al my kinrede in this place,
But I of him may gete bettre grace.
But nathelees, I wole of him assaye,   895
At certeyn dayes, yeer by yeer, to paye,
And thanke him of his grete curteisye.
My trouthe wol I kepe, I wol nat lie.'
   With herte soor he gooth unto his cofre,
And broghte gold unto this philosophre,   900
The value of five hundred pound, I gesse,
And him bisecheth, of his gentillesse,
To graunte him dayes of the remenaunt;
And seyde, 'Maister, I dar wel make avaunt,
I failled nevere of my trouthe as yit.   905
For sikerly my dette shal be quit
Towardes yow, howevere that I fare,
To goon a-begged in my kirtle bare.
But wolde ye vouche sauf, upon seuretee,
Two yeer or thre for to respiten me,   910
Thanne were I wel; for elles moot I selle
Myn heritage; ther is namoore to telle.'
   This philosophre sobrely answerde,
And seyde thus, whan he thise wordes herde:
'Have I nat holden covenant unto thee?'   915
   'Yes, certes, wel and trewely,' quod he.
   'Hastow nat had thy lady as thee liketh?'
   'No, no,' quod he, and sorwefully he siketh.
   'What was the cause? tel me if thou kan.'

- Chaucer does not seem to have written an account of how the Franklin's fellow travellers responded to his question. What is your view? Who has lost most, or sacrificed most? Is it more noble to sacrifice love than money? And what would some of the other pilgrims have thought? Consider the response of, for instance, the Squire (a romantic fellow), the Host, the Merchant or the Wife of Bath – all characters you encounter in the General Prologue. Is it significant that the Franklin asks only the males of the group (Lordynges) for their comment?
- Ending a story with an ethical question was common practice. The comparative status of a knight, a squire and a clerk would have relevance within the tale itself, and also for a man as conscious of the value of good behaviour and appearances as the Franklin narrator. But Chaucer is addressing a wider audience, and the 'journey' has deeper spiritual implications than the Canterbury journey that provides the framework for the tales. The significance of what makes a gentleman, a good person, someone 'fre' and 'gentil', was an important issue in the fourteenth century and has relevance for us today. 'Fre' was a word that implied a man's generous nature and unselfishness, but also suggested his social status – someone who was not 'bound' like a serf or peasant. What might the Franklin – one of the new, up and coming breed of men – hope to gain from telling such a tale? Is Chaucer using him to suggest the problems the old-fashioned 'courtly' ideals might face in the brash, modern world of the fourteenth century?

924	**Hadde levere** would rather	942–3	**As thou right … knowen me** as if you had just this moment sprung from the earth, and as if you had never known me before this moment [an abbreviated version of the formal quitclaim]
925	**fals** false		
926	**als** also		
927	**looth hire was** how unwilling she was		
929–30	**hir trouthe … of apparence** she made her promise in all innocence – she had never heard tell of illusions [apparitions]	945	**craft** skill
		945	**ne noght for my travaille** nor anything for my hard work
932	**right as frely** just as freely [generously]	946	**vitaille** food and drink [he has been provided for most hospitably]
935	**leeve brother** dear brother	947	**ynogh** enough
938–40	**God forbede … it is no drede** God forbid in all his heavenly power if a clerk cannot make a noble gesture as well as any of you, without doubt	949	**lordinges** my lords [the assembled pilgrims]
		951	**er that ye ferther wende** before you travel any further

Aurelius explains his position and the philosopher approves of the generous and noble natures displayed by both the squire and the knight. He too can do a 'gentil' deed, he says, and releases Aurelius from his debt.

Aurelius his tale anon bigan,   920
And tolde him al, as ye han herd bifoore;
It nedeth nat to yow reherce it moore.
    He seide, 'Arveragus, of gentillesse,
Hadde levere die in sorwe and in distresse
Than that his wyf were of hir trouthe fals.'   925
The sorwe of Dorigen he tolde him als;
How looth hire was to been a wikked wyf,
And that she levere had lost that day hir lyf,
And that hir trouthe she swoor thurgh innocence,—
She nevere erst hadde herd speke of apparence.   930
'That made me han of hire so greet pitee;
And right as frely as he sente hire me,
As frely sente I hire to him ageyn.
This al and som; ther is namoore to seyn.'
    This philosophre answerde, 'Leeve brother,   935
Everich of yow dide gentilly til oother.
Thou art a squier and he is a knight;
But God forbede, for his blisful might,
But if a clerk koude doon a gentil dede
As wel as any of yow, it is no drede!   940
    Sire, I releesse thee thy thousand pound,
As thou right now were cropen out of the ground,
Ne nevere er now ne haddest knowen me.
For, sire, I wol nat taken a peny of thee
For al my craft, ne noght for my travaille.   945
Thou hast ypayed wel for my vitaille.
It is ynogh, and farewel, have good day!'
And took his hors, and forth he goth his way.
Lordinges, this question, thanne, wol I aske now,
Which was the mooste fre, as thinketh yow?   950
Now telleth me, er that ye ferther wende.
I kan namoore; my tale is at an ende.

Chaucer's pilgrims

The Canterbury pilgrims leaving the Tabard Inn at Southwark

In order of appearance:

The Knight	brave, devout and unassuming – the perfect gentleman
The Squire	in training to follow in the knight, his father's, footsteps, a fine and fashionable young man, and madly in love
The Yeoman	the knight's only servant, a skilled bowman and forester
The Prioress	a most ladylike head of a nunnery; she takes great pains with her appearance and manners; she loves animals. She is accompanied by another nun and three priests, the nun and one priest also telling tales
The Monk	fine and prosperous looking, well-mounted; he loves hunting
The Friar	cheerful and sociable, he is skilled at obtaining alms from those he visits, particularly the ladies
The Merchant	rather secretive; his main interest is commerce
The Clerk	thin and shabby, his passion is scholarship; he spends all he has on books
The Sergeant at Law	a judge at the assize courts; one of the few pilgrims about whom Chaucer says very little
The Franklin	a wealthy and hospitable landowner and a JP; but not a member of the aristocracy
The Five Guildsmen	although they pursue different crafts or trades, they belong to the same social guild – rather self-important townsfolk
The Cook	he has been brought along to provide meals for the guildsmen; although he is a versatile cook, Chaucer suggests his personal hygiene could be improved
The Shipman	a weather-beaten master mariner

The Doctor of Physic	finely dressed and a skilled medical practitioner; he is an expert in astrology and natural magic; he loves gold
The Wife of Bath	skilled at weaving; her chief claim to fame is her five husbands
The Parson	the only truly devout churchman in Chaucer's group; he avoids all the tricks unscrupulous clerics used to get rich, and spends his care and energy on his parishioners
The Ploughman	the parson's brother and, like him, a simple, honest hard-working man
The Miller	tough, ugly and a cheat
The Manciple	responsible for organising the provisions for the lawyers in one of the Inns of Court – clearly a plum job for a clever man
The Reeve	unsociable, but able; the estate manager of a young nobleman
The Summoner	an official of a church court; corrupt, lewd and offensive
The Pardoner	another unpleasant churchman – he earns money by selling 'pardons' from Rome, and by letting simple folk see the fake holy relics he carries
The Host	the genial landlord of 'The Tabard', who accompanies them on the pilgrimage, and organises the story-telling
Geoffrey Chaucer	he depicts himself as rather shy and unassuming.

They are later joined by another story teller – **The Canon's Yeoman**, a servant whose tale betrays his master's obsessive interest in alchemy.

A modern pilgrim at Compostela, Spain

Pilgrims and pilgrimages

Pilgrimages are journeys made to sacred places, usually as acts of religious devotion. They became increasingly popular during the twelfth and thirteenth centuries, at the time when the threats to the Christian world from infidels and heathens from the east reached their height. The passion to defend and reaffirm the power of the Christian church manifested itself in Crusades to the Holy Land, and an upsurge in religious fervour. Shrines were established in many European countries in places of great religious significance. In England, Canterbury Cathedral was the site of the assassination of Archbishop Becket; Walsingham in Norfolk became a holy site of pilgrimage after visions of the Virgin Mary had been seen there. The great cathedral city of Cologne was another centre of pilgrimage, as was Compostela. Further afield, many pilgrims made the long journey to Jerusalem, available for visits from Christian pilgrims after the Emperor Frederick II had negotiated peace with the infidels, and had himself crowned king of the holy city.

Pilgrims (travelling in groups for companionship and safety) would travel to shrines at home and abroad to celebrate their devotion to the church, to seek pardon for their sins, and to ask favours of the saint whose relics were preserved in that place. The traditional image of a pilgrim is of one who travels humbly and simply, dressed in plain clothes, often on foot, carrying a staff. The emblem of a pilgrim is the scallop or cockle shell, worn on cap or hood. This was particularly the symbol of St James, patron saint of military crusaders, and the journey to his shrine in Compostela, northern Spain, was, and still is, one of the great pilgrim routes across Europe. The shells may originally have been real ones, but were later moulded in lead, as were most other pilgrim badges.

By the time Chaucer decided to use a group of pilgrims as a framework for his *Canterbury Tales*, reasons for pilgrimage had become less exclusively devotional. It was certainly a profitable business for enterprising people, as well as a popular pastime. The tourist industry began to take off. The Venetians offered a regular ferry service carrying travellers to and from the Holy Land. The monks of Cluny, the greatest religious house in France, ran a string of hostels along the entire route between their monastery and Compostela. Travel guides were produced, giving information about accommodation available along the route. One for Compostela contained useful Basque vocabulary, and a description of what to see in the cathedral. Horse dealers did a healthy trade hiring out horses to pilgrims.

There was great competition for popular relics between the religious establishments, which sometimes led to rather obvious forgeries. At least two places, for instance, claimed to possess the head of John the Baptist. Pilgrims began to bring home their own souvenirs, and to house them in their local churches, like the four-teenth century traveller William Wey, who proudly deposited in his Wiltshire village church his maps, a reproduction of St Veronica's handkerchief, which he had rubbed on the pillars of 'the tempyl of Jerusalem', and a large number of stones picked up in sites around the Holy Land. His parish priest was presumably delighted. Badges and emblems made of lead were sold at shrines, and eagerly purchased as souvenirs by travellers – the cockle shell for St James, the palm tree from Jericho. At Canterbury it was possible to buy an assortment of badges – an image of the head of the saint, St Thomas riding a horse, a little bell, or a small ampulla [bottle] to hold sacred water. Permission was given from Rome for the local religious houses to obtain a licence to manufacture these.

Some of Chaucer's pilgrims seem to have genuinely devout reasons for visiting Canterbury: the Knight, for instance, has come straight from his military expeditions abroad, fighting for Christendom, and his simple coat is still stained from its contact with his coat of mail. On the other hand, the Wife of Bath, although an enthusiastic pilgrim, hardly seems to be travelling in a spirit of piety or devotion. She lists the places she has visited like a seasoned traveller determined to visit as many tourist attractions as possible. By using a pilgrimage as the frame on which to hang his stories and characterisations, Chaucer was able to point out the way in which attitudes and standards were changing and old values were being lost.

Geoffrey Chaucer

Geoffrey Chaucer

BIOGRAPHICAL NOTES

1340?   The actual date of his birth is uncertain, but he was near 60 when he died. His father and grandfather were both vintners – wealthy London merchants, who supplied wines to the king's court.

Chaucer was introduced to court life in his teens. By the age of 16 he was employed in the service of the wife of the king's son, Lionel, later Duke of Clarence.

1359   He fought in France in the army of Edward III. He was captured and imprisoned, but released on payment of his ransom by the duke.

Chaucer was clearly valued by the king and other members of the royal family. In the **1360s** and **1370s** he was sent on diplomatic missions to France, Genoa, Florence and Lombardy.

1360s   He married Philippa de Roet, a maid-in-waiting to Edward III's wife, Queen Philippa. His wife's half-sister was Katherine Swynford, third wife of John of Gaunt. The link with this powerful Duke of Lancaster was an important one; the duke was Chaucer's patron and in later life gave Chaucer a pension of £10 a year.

1368?   Chaucer wrote *The Book of the Duchess*, a poem on the death of the Duchess Blanche, first wife of John of Gaunt.

1374   The position of Comptroller of Customs for the port of London was given to Chaucer, and in the same year the king granted him a pitcher of wine daily. Other lucrative administrative posts became his later.

1374?   Chaucer began his unfinished work *The House of Fame*.

1382?   Chaucer wrote *The Parlement of Fowles* – possibly for the marriage of Richard II.

1386   Like the Franklin in *The Canterbury Tales*, Chaucer was appointed 'Knight of the Shire' or Parliamentary representative for the county of Kent.

Early 1380s He wrote *Troilus and Criseyde*.

It seems that, in spite of the royal and noble patronage he enjoyed, Chaucer was an extravagant man, and money slipped through his fingers. In 1389 he was appointed Clerk of the King's Works by Richard II, but the position lasted only two years.

Richard later gave him a pension of £20 for life, which Chaucer frequently asked for 'in advance'. Threats of arrest for non-payment of debts were warded off by letters of protection from the crown.

c. 1388   Chaucer probably began to formulate his ideas for *The Canterbury Tales* around this time.

1391   He was appointed deputy forester (an administrative post) in Petherton, Somerset, and may have spent some time there.

| 1399 | Henry IV, son of John of Gaunt, became king, and Chaucer was awarded a new pension of 40 marks (about £26), which allowed him to live his few remaining months in comfort. |
| 1400 | Chaucer died in October, and was buried in Westminster Abbey. |

CHAUCER THE WRITER AND SCHOLAR

Geoffrey Chaucer was actively involved in diplomatic life, moving in court circles, and travelling extensively; he was also an extremely well-read man. His writing shows the influence of classical authors, as well as more recent French and Italian works. The wide range of biblical, classical and contemporary literary references in *The Canterbury Tales*, especially in the Wife of Bath's Prologue and Tale, bear witness to his learning, and he confesses to owning 60 books – a very considerable library in those days. Many of the ideas and themes which occur in *The Canterbury Tales* have been adapted from the works of classical and contemporary sources known to Chaucer and to at least some of his audiences. His earliest works, such as *The Book of the Duchess*, show the influence of courtly and allegorical French love poetry, in particular the *Roman de la Rose*, a dream poem about the psychology of falling in love. *The Book of the Duchess* is a dream poem in this tradition.

The House of Fame, an unfinished narrative poem, shows influences from Chaucer's reading in Italian as well as French poetry. Chaucer is almost the only writer of the century outside Italy to show knowledge of the *Divine Comedy* of Dante (1265–1321), but in this poem, he challenges Dante's claim that it is possible to know the truth about people's actions and motives in the past. Chaucer also admired the writings of two other Italians, Petrarch and Boccaccio; the latter's *Decameron* employs the linking device (in his case a group of sophisticated men and women, entertaining one another with story-telling in a country retreat, whilst the Black Death rages in Florence) that Chaucer was to use later with far greater subtlety, variety and skill.

In both *Troilus and Criseyde,* a re-telling of the tale of love and betrayal at the time of the Trojan War, and in *The Canterbury Tales,* Chaucer shows the debt he owed to classical writers, in particular Ovid and Virgil. He was also familiar with the Bible and some of the writings of theologians highly respected in the Middle Ages, such as St Jerome and St Augustine. He greatly admired the Roman philosopher Boethius, whose work *De Consolatione Philosophiae* (The Consolation of Philosophy) he translated from its original Latin into English. His writing shows an interest in astronomy and astrology, and he wrote one of the very first textbooks in English, *A Treatise on the Astrolabe,* explaining the workings of this astronomical instrument for 'little Lewis', presumably a young son who died in infancy – we hear nothing of him later.

Symbolism in the Franklin's Tale

THE BLACK ROCKS AND THE COURTLY GARDEN

We see the black rocks off the coast of Brittany very much through Dorigen's eyes, and indeed through her own words. They are coloured by her fears for her husband and the safety of her marriage. Her response to them is emotional and it follows from this that the description is powerful and dramatic. The adjectives used suggest evil associations: they are 'black', 'feendly', 'foul'; the whole tone and thrust of Dorigen's speech is forceful and violent, as she questions the value of such dangerous things, which promote such a strong emotional response in her. The rocks symbolise hidden and half-hidden dangers that could separate Dorigen and her husband from one another. It doesn't matter that her hatred of them is irrational – they represent her fear that something could endanger her marriage. She feels helpless when faced with their power and malignant force. Her fear is so great that she steps outside the natural bounds of orthodox religion and questions why God should have created such things. He is supposed to love mankind, and yet He puts such ugly and apparently purposeless threatening things in His world. They do not fit in with her idea of an ordered universe – if God planned the world, how could He create such an ugly, disordered chaos, how do such things fit into His divine plan? She can only ask – she cannot see.

It is exactly because of her strong love for her husband and her fear for his safety that she makes her foolish promise to Aurelius, and it is, of course, this promise that creates the hidden dangers upon which her marriage nearly founders. The rocks – part of God's natural universe – do not really disappear, although they seem to. Her rebellious questioning of God's order has led her into dangerous waters, and when she learns that the rocks have 'disappeared' she perversely sees their absence as 'unnatural' and wishes for their return. Only the great 'gentillesse' and generosity of the knight and the squire can restore tranquillity and happiness and order to Dorigen's universe.

By contrast, we learn about the garden through the 'author's voice'. It seems at first simply part of the story, the next setting in the tale. Even so, there is a definite suggestion that this is a pleasant place. Descriptive words are softer and more gentle; the garden is far more in keeping with gentle early summer – a place of growth and flowering and beauty, refreshed by natural showers and warm suns.

Described immediately after the introduction of the fearful rocks, the garden is a model of order and harmony – an orderliness emphasised by Chaucer's mention of the board games of chess and backgammon, both of which rely heavily on a sense of pattern and rule (invented and imposed by man). The garden, too, has been carefully 'wrought' and crafted. We are reminded of order through description of the patterned 'dance' and by the patterns of flowers and leaves to be seen.

However, the garden – as the reader is most carefully told – has been made by man out of God's natural gifts. Man has imposed the order upon nature. Although it might seem eminently suitable as a place for play and entertainment – not half so threatening as the natural power of the rocks – the order has been imposed by man's

'They dauncen, and they pleyen at ches and tables'

hand, not God's. It may be, therefore, that this harmony, and tamed nature is an illusion, not reality. To emphasise the hidden dangers lurking beneath this serene exterior, we are told, moreover, that this garden is as fair as the Garden of Eden – where foolish woman was tempted into doing something wrong, in the belief that it might benefit herself and her mate. The parallel with Dorigen is clear. Chaucer has alerted us in both descriptions to the idea of rules – God's rules and man's rules; to things that seem harmful and harmless, and to hidden dangers. He has taken a story about love between men and women and given it an added dimension.

Literary devices

RHETORIC

The ability to speak eloquently in public, to argue lucidly and inform one's audience entertainingly and effectively was extremely important in an age when many were unable to read and write. Rhetoric was one of the seven liberal arts taught at medieval universities (the others were Grammar, Logic, Music, Arithmetic, Geometry and Astronomy) and people with the most basic education would be expected to understand the formalities of rhetorical speech. Narrators who wished to tell their stories properly, particularly if they were dealing with formal, moral or serious subject matter, would use the 'rules' or 'flowers' of rhetoric in their narration. These are the rules the Franklin refers to in his prologue, and Chaucer, his creator, allows the way he talks of them to give us a fuller understanding of his character and attitudes. Many of the devices he uses have precise names and functions:

diminutio beginning one's narration with an apology for one's lack of ability
interpretatio saying the same thing more than once in different words

85

circumlocutio	saying or hinting at something obliquely (for example, the Franklin's statement that he 'never slept on Mount Parnassus' in line 49 means he has no knowledge of the Muse of literature, whose home was Parnassus in classical mythology)
adnominatio	the use of metaphorical devices – such as 'flowers' or 'colours' when applied to rhetoric.

This introductory passage would alert Chaucer's audience to the manner in which the tale was to be told; it is also the first indication that what the Franklin says and what he means or believes are not necessarily the same thing. Chaucer himself was far too skilled an author to make an obvious display of his rhetorical skills, but his use of them in this tale adds extra dimensions both to the content of the tale itself and the desire of its teller to be recognised as a member of the upper classes. Other indications of rhetorical display abound:

diversio	digression – such as the Franklin's words about marriage in general beginning line 89
sententia	a moral comment about life and behaviour
exclamatio	a lament intended to express to the audience the emotional state of a character
exemplum	the use of an example from literature which offers a comparison with the situation of the character in the tale.

THE BRETON LAY

If the Franklin wished to find a type of story most appropriate to his courtly aspirations, then the Breton lay was very suitable. Literature of the twelfth century abounded with such lays, which were romantic stories of chivalry, magic and courtly love, the best known being those collected or created by the French poet Marie de France. It would seem, therefore, that by setting his tale in Dorigen's native Brittany and choosing material about lovers and their beautiful ladies, the Franklin has provided an impeccable pedigree for this tale of Dorigen, Aurelius and Arveragus. He has chosen as his source an old-fashioned genre enjoyed by a privileged elite. In fact, Chaucer's discerning audience would quickly be made aware of the differences between this source and the tale being told. First, although traditional lays were set in imaginary countries far away, the idea of using a Breton story allows Chaucer to set his tale in a real place he apparently knows very well, even to a knowledge of the effects of spring tides. An important link between reality and this fantasy tale is thus established. (This 'foreign' setting also allows Chaucer to distance himself from the magical element disapproved of by the fourteenth century church. After all, he might argue, what could one expect from foreigners in the previous century?) Secondly, although the lays were often about emotions and often focused on the lady, this tale, instead of ending with a fairy tale marriage, begins with one. The magic in the lays of Marie de France was usually concerned with the inexplicable and supernatural, yet here the illusion of disappearing rocks is firmly linked to the 'natural' magic of studying the movement of the planets and the resulting high tides.

COURTLY LOVE

The whole issue of courtly love is called to question by Chaucer's story. The game of courtly love involved an elaborate pattern of behaviour in which a young man acted towards the lady of his choice with extreme respect – almost worship. The devout adoration given to the lady of a noble knight's choice mirrored (or even replaced) the adoration of the Virgin Mary so central to the religious life of the Christian world. During the courtship, or game of love, she was always in the superior position. Her 'suitor' performed all manner of brave and foolhardy deeds to gain her notice, and would suffer the pangs of unrequited love patiently and hopelessly until such time as she was moved to show pity or concern towards him. At no time would he expect her to reward him with sexual favours. Should such secret and painful passion eventually be returned by the lady, and should she be in a position to accept it, the knight might then be lucky enough to marry her. After marriage, positions would be reversed. The husband would assume control of his wife, and her fidelity and meek subservience would be considered a foregone conclusion (though in real life, presumably, this was not always the way she behaved). If the lady of his choice was already married to someone else (as was often the case) in theory at least the relationship was supposed to remain in a secret and static state of unrequited love. Chaucer considers the theme of courtly love twice in this tale, in the relationships between Dorigen and both men, and invites us to consider how such an elevated and unreal game can function within the real world.

This tournament shield illustrates the idea of courtly love. The young knight kneels to his beautiful lady; he is dressed for battle, helmet by his side and death at his back – a reminder of the dangers he is prepared to face for her sake

The changing world of Chaucer's England

In the early Middle Ages there had been considerable social stability. A man's status clarified his privileges and responsibilities. By the late fourteenth century the stable framework of society had become remarkably fluid. It was no longer possible to classify all members of society adequately within the confines of the three estates (or social classes), defined below.

The nobility Those entitled to bear arms and responsible for the protection of the whole community. They owned lands, lived in castles, owed loyalty to their overlords and were themselves supported in peace and war both by inferiors in the knightly scale and by the peasants who were their tenants. An individual knight might own a small patch of scrubby, worthless pasture and a draughty, dilapidated ancestral home in the more remote part of the country, but if he could trace his descent from a noble family, he too was 'noble'. He was entitled to bear arms on his shield and his standard, and expected to bear sword and shield on horseback into battle should the greater noble, to whom he owed fealty, require this of him.

The clergy Priests, monks, nuns and friars took responsibility for the spiritual welfare of all. Formal education was almost exclusively in the hands of monastic and church schools, so that most literate members of society were connected to the church. They instructed and informed the rest of the population, high and low, acted as scribes, clerks and administrators, and maintained a perpetual background of prayer for the spiritual health of the other two estates.

The peasants As the country was predominantly agricultural, the labourers mainly worked the fields, tending their lord's lands and animals as well as their own small-holdings. The lowest were serfs, with no personal rights at all – they could be sold, as slaves or cattle might be sold. They were not allowed to move off the lord's land without his permission. Their children became his property.

Of course, there had always been blurred edges to these sharp distinctions. Peasants could buy their freedom; some became relatively wealthy and acquired substantial land holdings. Some clerks chose to leave the church and devote their time to legal matters, or administration in the service of wealthy nobles, or even the king. Some religious houses were larger and owned more estates than many of the nobility, and in their turn needed to employ the services of peasants. Some knights were not interested in managing their own estates and left their property in the hands of shrewd men of business who might have come originally from peasant stock.
But by the late fourteenth century, people felt it necessary to define the increasingly complex social groups, and many whose families who had not originally been 'gentil' adopted the lifestyle, habits and attributes formerly the exclusive preserve of the knightly class.

Black Death and its aftermath

One of the fundamental causes of change was the Black Death, which reached England in 1348, to return with only slightly less virulence in 1361 and 1368. In 1346 came stories of a terrible, unstoppable plague devastating Asia and India. Within a year, merchant ships from the Levant and the Crimean peninsula brought the sickness to Sicily, Genoa and Venice, and by the 1350s between one-third and half of the population had died, not only in England, but everywhere between Iceland and India. Widespread and terrifying devastation led to a time of economic and social chaos.

As a semblance of normality returned to the depleted population, many found their first chance to break free from constricting bonds of serfdom, and the opportunity to become landowners. Deserted villages, half empty estates, lack of peasants to work fields and run farms meant that labourers commanded high wages, whilst land prices were low. Cheap land was available for the taking. Shrewd intelligent peasants seized their opportunities. Richer peasants had the skills and opportunities to run small estates; various degrees of peasantry merged into one another: at the top end they became wealthy tenant farmers. The term 'yeoman' applied equally to rich tenants and freehold-owning franklins. In time, such men could aspire to become 'gentry'. After the plague years, shrewd franklins took up land leases on estates previously owned by 'noble' families.

The impact of Richard II

The influence of a cultured and literate king did much in itself to encourage the blurring of distinctions between nobility and other ranks. Only 11 when he became king in 1377, as a young man Richard brought an air of French sophistication to the English throne, introducing such refinements as the fork, and extraordinary little things known as handkerchiefs ('little pieces of cloth for giving to the lord King for carrying in his hand for wiping and cleansing his nose').

Richard II gathered around him not just court officials but a more fluid and informal group of talented people, who shared his wide interests – religion, history, hunting, good food, astrology, and poetry. Encouraged by him, exquisite works were achieved by people like the master carver William Wynford, and the painter of the Wilton Diptych. Geoffrey Chaucer was not the only court poet; French writers such as Froissart, were honoured by Richard, as well as the English Gower. People with talent, culture and ability were as likely to be favoured by this king as members of the old aristocracy, able to trace their lineage through several generations.

Furthermore, influence from the splendid and wealthy courts of the Italian states, was also blurring the distinction between a nobleman and someone who possessed riches, good taste and intelligence, but did not necessarily come from an aristocratic background. The Italian ruling classes and 'gentility' had different credentials. Wealthy Italian patrons of the arts were often merchants and business men with cultivated tastes – and when they met the 'old' gentility of other nations they expected to be treated as equals.

The effects of the Peasants' Revolt

One issue raised by the Peasants' Revolt of 1381 was the vexed question of why some men should consider themselves superior to others. One of Wat Tyler's demands at Smithfield was that 'no lord should have lordship in future, but it should be divided among all men, except for the king's own lordship … 'He demanded there should be 'no more villeins in England, and no serfdom nor villeinage, but that all men should be free and of one condition. '

Once the upheaval of the revolt had died down, the authorities desperately scrambled to reinstate the divisions of society, and those privileges previously enjoyed by 'gentil' folk. In November 1381 the promise made to Wat Tyler and his army was repudiated by Parliament: 'they (prelates, commons, lords) prayed humbly to our lord the king that as these letters of manumission and enfranchisement had been made and granted through coercion, to the disinheritance of themselves and the destruction of the realm, they should be wiped out and annulled by the authority of this parliament.' Clearly, the old aristocracy intended to hang on to its status and privileges for as long as possible. But in an age when culture and refinement were becoming increasingly important aspects of 'gentilesse', the question 'What is a gentle, or a noble person?' was repeatedly debated.

Gentillesse

WHAT WAS IT?

Gentillesse was traditionally a code of behaviour or way of life associated with the noble (and knightly) class, and included a number of qualities: generosity, chivalrous or gentlemanly deeds, bravery, social graces, delicacy of feeling, integrity (a gentleman's word is his bond – very relevant in this tale), and many others.

WHO POSSESSED IT?

A person was considered to be of 'gentle' or 'noble' birth if he:
   a)   came from a family that owned land
   b)   bore arms
   c)   was relatively wealthy.

He was expected to fight on horseback, hunt, ride, hawk and so forth and to be able to sing, write songs, dance, and joust. The Knight and Squire of the General Prologue between them embody most of these qualities. But a man could appear to be 'gentil' if he wore fine clothes and possessed some or most of the qualities of the noble class.

Not every member of the noble classes could qualify as a gentleman on all the above counts: some were poor, had lost lands and fortune; others were totally boorish, or immoral; others exceedingly stupid; some did not wish to become fighting men. Nevertheless, men who were descended from the old landed, noble families, considered themselves to be 'gentil' and qualified to wear a coat of arms.

They could be clearly nobles: members of wealthy and powerful families that had owned land for many generations – frequently with influence at court, often advisors to the king, and maintainers of their own bands of fighting men. Or they might be knights, a more general and all-embracing term. There could be rich knights and poor ones, and sometimes they held the bulk of their land as tenants of some greater lord or noble. Then there were squires, often (and for the purposes of this tale) the sons of knights, hoping to 'win their spurs' and become knights themselves.

WHERE DID FRANKLINS FIT IN?

A franklin was a landowner who could not trace his descent from those of noble birth. Perhaps he had seized the opportunity to acquire a land holding after the Black Death. He might well be richer than some knights, more educated, more sophisticated, might hold local offices (knight of the shire, sheriff etc.) but he was not of 'noble' blood, and therefore some might consider him to be inferior.

Consequently, a franklin might well wish to prove himself just as good, as worthy and as 'gentil' as a knight or a squire. He might have ambitions for later generations of his own family to keep climbing the social ladder (like the Franklin in *The Canterbury Tales* has for his son). He would use his dress, lifestyle and behaviour to indicate that he was a gentleman.

Another way to improve himself was through education. As literacy spread and embraced areas other than strictly religious ones, merchants, lawyers, franklins and wealthier peasants began to enjoy a more cultured lifestyle. Books on hunting, for example, though often written by nobles, were popular at all levels of society; London book owners included vintners, merchants, and lawyers.

'GENTILLESSE' AND THE FRANKLIN'S TALE

The question of 'gentillesse' was a burning issue, and one which Chaucer himself discussed more than once in his writings. His views were close to those of Boethius and Dante, two writers he clearly revered, who had written on the same issue. In an early ballad *Gentillesse* he saw this quality as a personal one, not hereditary – claimants to gentillesse should follow Christ's example in their behaviour. Virtue was the source of dignity, not the other way round. A 'vicious' man – someone ignoble or ungentlemanly – could just as easily be the product of a noble family as the son of a rough villein or peasant. Gentility, Chaucer said, has to do with one's way of life. The characteristics of gentility were righteousness, truth, freedom – and only if one's heirs followed the same path could they be considered truly 'gentil'.

Could a man become noble?

Like Chaucer himself, the Franklin of this tale is a member of the middle classes – a free man, not a knight. Although he holds a number of county offices, and keeps company with the Sergeant at Law – unquestionably a superior personage – those offices he has are those of a minor official. His attitude to the Squire suggests admiration for a sort of indefinable charisma he himself would like to possess. It would be several years before families like the Franklin's could really call themselves gentlemen. Money, though important, was not everything. In the late fourteenth century, franklins were feathering their nests by enlarging their land holdings and gaining power in areas where the local aristocrats were weak or few. Ultimately their hopes lay with their sons – and that is why this franklin is so pre-occupied with his son and his son's progress.

Chaucer's Franklin, though not a 'gentil' man, is clearly prosperous and longs to be recognised as a person of social standing. Chaucer depicts him as constantly aware of the 'proper' things to do and say, and the 'right' way to behave. In this way the writer is poking sly fun at his creation. Our Franklin wants to prove himself a man of great sensibility, who knows how the upper class behaves, and Chaucer draws the reader's attention to this on several occasions. His attitude towards the Squire, and the Host, and his concerns about his own son have already been mentioned. His decision to tell what is apparently a Breton lay – with the veneer of old-fashioned refinement such a tale would have had – allows him to tell of fantasy and courtly love, the bravest knights, most excellent squires and beautiful ladies. All of these are bound by codes of conduct associated with 'gentillesse'. Occasionally Chaucer encourages his audience to question the probability of their behaviour at times when common sense suggest it is absurd.

Finally, however, the Franklin and his creator speak as one. 'Fre' or generous behaviour is shown to be a quality possessed by a generous and hospitable clerk, as readily as by a knight or squire. 'Gentillesse' is concerned with behaviour and virtue, rather than class, as this tale ultimately reveals.

Astronomy and astrology in the Franklin's Tale

Although today the gulf between astronomy and astrology appears enormous, in Chaucer's lifetime the distinction between these two branches of study might initially have seemed insignificant. Astronomy is the scientific study of stars, planets and the universe; astrology, according to one dictionary, is 'the primitive study of astronomy'. But more importantly, astrology is also called 'the study of the relative positions of moon, stars and planets, interpreted in terms of human characteristics and activities'. Astrologers attempted to foretell the future of men by studying the movements in the heavens. In other words, although an astronomer is a reputable and distinguished scientist, an astrologer could well be called a magician, a dabbler in the black arts, or a charlatan.

By the fourteenth century, there had been great discoveries in many areas: measurement of heights by triangulation; the invention of eyeglasses; the manufacture of paper (with widespread effects on the spread of information). There was also increased awareness of the movement of planets and the effect of sun and moon on tides and weather, as well as fascinated speculation about other effects this heavenly movement might have on the world below. Universities specialised in particular branches of knowledge (Bologna for law, Paris for theology) but an initial course of study at any one of the great universities was based on the seven liberal arts, and of these astronomy was generally considered the most rigorous, arcane and spiritually challenging branch of study. Astronomers traced the regularities and irregularities of movement in the heavens, and recognised these as a manifest indication of the structure of the universe. They believed that by studying the movement of planets they could predict and foretell tragedies on a global and personal scale, and explain things otherwise incomprehensible.

One of the great astronomers of the age was Nicolas Oresme, advisor to Charles V of France, a true scientific researcher with a healthy contempt for superstition. He exemplified the pursuit of knowledge in a fast-changing world. But his attitude was at odds with that of many for whom study of the stars was rather a branch of black magic. The cataclysmic effect of the Black Death had brought with it a wave of hysteria and superstition, augmented by a growing cynicism towards the Christian church. It was often seen as corrupt in its practices and, after the Schism of 1375

Medieval man reaches out from his own world in an attempt to understand the secrets of the universe

during which there was bloody fighting between the supporters of two rival popes, leaderless. This lack of strong leadership under a firm papacy lasted from the mid-1370s until after the end of the century. 'Truly,' said one chronicler in 1375 'it seems as if these times are under the rule of a planet which produces strife and quarrelling … truly the whole world is become a valley of shadows.'

There were many who believed in magic as a powerful force in the world. Certainly, the idea that a man's behaviour and the very nature of his personality were influenced by the time and place of his birth, was fundamental to much medieval thought. The king of France admired the scientist Nicholas Oresme, but he also employed a court astrologer, Thomas of Pisano. In spite of the fact that the church hated the influence of fortune-tellers and astrologers, at least one pope was treated by a physician who practised in accordance with guidance from his studies of the zodiac (Guy de Chauliac).

The Franklin's Tale reflects the ambivalence of the age. On the one hand, the Franklin (and his creator) reveals considerable expertise and understanding of the movement of planets. On the other, this is confusedly linked to a use of magical arts which are in some way alien to Christian beliefs. The attitude towards the knowledgeable clerk is both admiring and disapproving. In spite of being impressed by his magical skills, the Franklin, as a Christian, is at pains to voice his contempt for such 'tregetours'.

Themes in the Franklin's Tale

1 THE IMPORT OF THE TALE

a) Promises – who makes them, who keeps them, why are they made and with what consequences?

b) Characters – what do we learn about all four characters in The Franklin's Tale through their actions and their speeches, and what do we learn about the Franklin himself, from the choice and content of his Tale and its telling?

c) Medieval life and attitudes – how did people spend their time (from gambling, backgammon, home magic shows, and 'falling in love' to knightly expeditions).

2 RELATIONSHIPS BETWEEN MEN AND WOMEN

a) Is the marriage between Dorigen and Arveragus really an ideal and equal partnership? How much power does Dorigen really have? Is she given 'fredom' and, if so, does she use it well or is she simply the passive love object in a man's world?

b) How relevant is the content of The Franklin's Tale nowadays?

c) Can a man be both 'servant in love' and 'lord in mariage'?

d) Is it possible to apply idealistic conventions of romantic love to everyday life? Can similar courtship rituals, games and conventions be detected in modern society?

3 RELIGION

a) What did Chaucer's contemporaries believe in?

b) What do we learn about magic and astrology from The Franklin's Tale?

c) Why has Chaucer chosen to set this tale in pagan times – and are there episodes which seem more Christian than pagan?

d) What sort of moral codes are revealed?

4 THE WAY THE TALE IS TOLD

a) What do these abstract words mean: 'trouthe', 'honour', 'gentilesse', 'love', 'generosity' and how does the tale suggest different interpretations of them? For example, 'gentilesse' could be explored by asking: what is it? who possesses it? who aspires to it? is it just a fantasy? does wealth have anything to do with it?

b) What happens when people use words rashly and thoughtlessly? Consider Dorigen's promise to Aurelius and Aurelius' promise to the clerk.

c) How does a person's manner of speech reveals their inner wishes? Consider the Franklin's 'cultured' choice of tale and manner of its telling; Dorigen's expression of anxiety about her husband, and the task she sets for Aurelius.

d) How are the rules of rhetoric used in this tale not just to enhance the story-telling, but also to make subtle points about the content?

e) Why choose a 'Breton lay'? Why make Dorigen's lament so long? Why incorporate the description of the turning of the year?

f) Are we meant to take the behaviour of the main characters seriously at all times? Does Chaucer satirise their behaviour – including that of the Franklin?

5 APPEARANCE AND REALITY

The Franklin's Tale emphasises the fluidity of the natural world – the changing nature of things, of people's attitudes to one another and to life. Moral standpoints are undermined and questioned as the tale unfolds.

a) Are there indications that the attitudes of Chaucer and his narrator, the Franklin, are sometimes at variance? A thoughtful reading will bring out a number of points for discussion, some of which have already been mentioned. such as the nature of magic and love.

b) What is a 'gentil' man? Does it matter whether he is called knight, squire or clerk, magician or philosopher, gentleman, franklin or master?

Use these questions as a basis for written work or class discussion.

Glossary of frequently-used words

anlaas	small dagger	noght	nothing
anon	immediately	noon	no-one
aventure	chance, fate	paraventure	perhaps
biforn	in front of	pardee	*par Dieu* [by God]
biheste	promise [n]	partrich	partridge
bihight	promise [v]	passinge	better than
cleped	called, named	plentevous	plentiful
delit	pleasure, enjoyment	prively	privately, secretly
discrive	describe	quod	said, spoke
dorste	dared	semed	seemed
doun	down	seyde	said
eek	also	sholde	should
entendeth	attends, pays attention	sith	since
er	before	sodenly	suddenly
ese	comfort	sooth/sothe	truth
everichon	everyone	soper	supper
gipser	purse	swich	such
girdel	girdle or sash	thanne	then
greet	great	therwith	furthermore
han	have	thilke	this same
hem	them	tweye	two
housholdere	owner/ master of large household	vavasour	great landowner
		vouche sauf	grant, give permission
maistrie	mastery, control	wight	person
moot	must	wiste	knew, understood
morwe	morning	wone	custom, habit
muwe	coop or cage	woot	know, understand
nathelees	nevertheless	wroghte	wrought, performed
ne	neither/nor		